Next Level Ukulele

Easy play-along guide to understanding music,
building confidence and learning to jam like a pro,
with over 100 audio practice tracks

by David Shipway

Next Level Ukulele
by David Shipway

Published by Headstock Books
headstockbooks.com

Cover images by Samuel Ramos and Jakob Owens.

Paperback ISBN: 978-1-914453-75-5
Hardcover ISBN: 978-1-914453-77-9 / 978-1-914453-78-6
Ebook ISBN: 978-1-914453-76-2

Acknowledgements

There are a few people I would like to thank for their help in producing this, my second book for ukulele players.

Firstly, my son, James Shipway, for editing this book, contributing ideas and knowledge, and helping to make the content as informative as possible without getting too technical. James is a graduate of The Guitar Institute and Leeds College of Music and has a large following as a guitar teacher and author of books and courses for guitar players.

I also have to thank Aileen for all her work in the production, marketing and publishing side of things, and Jackie for her help in proof-reading and formatting.

I'd like to thank all those people who gave us such positive feedback in their reviews of my first book, *Music Theory for Ukulele*. This has been a great encouragement to press on with a second book.

Many of the ideas in this book have been tried and tested on students and members of the Uke'n'Play group, so thanks to these 'guinea pigs' for their patience and encouragement.

Finally, thank you to all those great musicians I've had the good fortune to meet, play with and learn from over the years.

David

Contents

Introduction

Hello and welcome to *Next Level Ukulele*!

If you want to take your ukulele skills to the next level by being able to *hear* and *understand* more about the music you play, especially when playing with others, then this book is for you.

The ukulele is a very sociable instrument. There are many ukulele groups out there to join, and no matter where in the world you live, there is likely one near to you. These provide a great opportunity for people of all ages and musical backgrounds to get together and have fun making music.

The thing is, as the leader of one such group, I've seen how easy it is for players to get stuck in a 'rut'. They become totally dependent on a chord sheet or songbook. In fact they're unable to play without it, let alone spontaneously 'jump in' and play along with others when the opportunity arises.

Friends in the group often tell me how frustrating this is! Perhaps you feel the same way? You've learned a load of chords, you can strum and change between them, why can't you put them together 'on the spot' to play along with other musicians at open-mic nights and other musical gatherings?

The good news is you can learn to do this - all it takes is a bit of knowledge, patience and practice. I aim to give you the knowledge in this book, patience and practice is down to you!

In my ukulele group I often hear the comment:

I can hear the chords changing but I don't know where they are going!

It's exactly this problem that we are going to address in **Next Level Ukulele**. With an understanding of some basic music theory and by practicing the right things in the right way, you'll be surprised to find you can overcome this problem. You'll also be amazed by the difference improving your listening skills, even just a bit, will make to your all-round ability as a uke player.

By giving you straightforward explanations, exercises and examples, I hope to provide you with a 'roadmap' for building a connection between what you *hear* in the music you play and how it relates to the ukulele.

If you follow the method in this book, then your musical 'ear' and your listening skills will improve dramatically. This will help you follow and remember the chords in the songs you play, recognise common chords and progressions, and play along with other musicians more confidently and more easily than ever before.

Eventually, you may even feel confident enough to jump in and play with others whenever you want to, *even* if they're playing music you haven't played before! This might seem like a terrifying scenario right now, but with what this book teaches you, it's something you can learn to do.

Get your free 'Play-Along' tracks!

The aim of this book is *not* to teach you music theory - I already did that in my ***Music Theory for Ukulele*** book, so see that for more in-depth music theory lessons. Although we will be covering some important theory topics, ***Next Level Ukulele*** is more about ***playing*** and ***listening*** than it is about reading.

Play the practical examples, *listen* carefully to the sound of them, and *explore* the material I show you using your ukulele and your *ears* – it's *not* just about me giving you information.

Make working through ***Next Level Ukulele*** a practical, 'play-along' process!

Do this, and it can have a **big** impact on your playing skills. You see, you're not just *reading* about the ukulele, you're actually working on building your practical skills.

To help you do this, I've created **audio demonstrations** and play-along **backing tracks** for you to use.

These will help you to *hear* what various concepts and exercises sound like, but they're also designed for **YOU** to **play-along** with on your ukulele. This will do wonders for your ukulele skills because you'll be growing your chord shape vocabulary, strumming, changing between chords, keeping your place in a piece of music... and much more besides.

Most of the tracks have a 'live band' feel, making them a lot of fun to play along with. They also give you a great way to realistically simulate a musical environment where you might play, for instance a ukulele club or band.

You need these audio tracks to get the most out of the book, so go to the following webpage and tell me the email address you'd like them sent to.

Get your FREE Play-Along audio tracks here:

headstockbooks.com/uke

On many tracks, you'll hear me playing the exercise a few times over the backing track. Then I drop out, leaving **you** to carry on alone (this is great practice for you!).

Don't forget these tracks, they're an essential part of the musical journey we're about to go on together, so go to the webpage given and grab them today.

How Should You Use This Book?

Follow these 6 simple tips to get the best possible results from ***Next Level Ukulele***:

1. Start at the beginning and work through the chapters in order. I've tried to build the content chapter by chapter - going through each one in sequence will make sure there are no gaps in your knowledge

2. Test yourself with the quiz at the end of each chapter to make sure you've understood everything. Then check your answers alongside those given and go back over anything you are not sure of

3. As I said earlier, this book is teaching you a practical skill, so make sure to do all the practical exercises I give you. Most of these can be played along with the **downloadable audio examples**

4. Take your time with this material. There's no rush, so go back over anything as many times as necessary. Some of the concepts and skills outlined take time to absorb and learn. You'll need to put a bit of time in before experiencing the 'light-bulb moment'!

5. Listen to the well-known song examples I suggest throughout the book. Leave aside your musical preferences for the moment and treat them as part of a learning process. I've selected them because they demonstrate something which we're discussing. Just a note about these suggestions, the original recordings may not always be in the same key as the examples in the book, sometimes I've chosen to move things into 'uke-friendly' keys

6. All examples assume you are using the standard ukulele tuning **G-C-E-A**

One More Important Tip: Listen and Hear!

To get good at playing along with other musicians you need to practice **LISTENING** and **HEARING**.

Sounds obvious doesn't it?

Here's the thing though - I don't just mean 'hearing' the sound you're making on your uke in a passive kind of way. I'm talking about really *listening* in a more focused way than you're maybe used to, so that you really start to *absorb* the sounds you're making on the instrument. Doing this will strengthen your musical ear, and with practice you'll be able to recognise and understand more of the music you play just from the sound of it.

To help you do this, try my 'PLAY, LISTEN, HEAR' method for the exercises and examples in this book:

1. PLAY the exercise on your uke

2. As you do this, really LISTEN to the characteristic sound and features of the example

3. Now *without* playing it, try to HEAR the sound in your head. Imagine what it would sound like if you *were* playing it

4. Repeat over and over!

Experiment with this approach for each exercise, it'll help you to focus on the **sound** instead of just what your fingers are doing. With time you'll be amazed how much your 'listening powers' grow, and how much this benefits you as a player.

To repeat what I said earlier, this is the main difference between this book and many other books out there. You see, I don't just want to give you more information, I want to help you learn to **notice and recognise** the things you hear in the music you're playing. Using this simple practice approach will help you to do this.

Ok, I think we're ready to get started...

So grab your uke, get in tune, and get ready for ***Next Level Ukulele***!

Chapter 1: Melody, Harmony, Chords and More!

To start with, we're going to cover some simple ideas to do with playing songs and chords on the uke. These concepts are important, and will help you to understand and get the very most out of this book.

If you know this material already, then great, it'll serve as a useful reminder of some basic but important musical knowledge. If you don't, then this chapter will help you to fill in some of the knowledge gaps you have as a player and musician.

Note: We're not going to go *really* deep into these concepts, so if you're completely new to music theory and how it relates to the uke, then you might also want to check out my *Music Theory for Ukulele* book for more information on the basics. This is the perfect way to fill in any knowledge gaps you might have.

So grab your uke and we'll get started...

The Basics

When we are strumming along to a song, we are basically providing a background to a tune or melody. It may be a vocal song or an instrumental piece, it doesn't matter.

What does matter is that the background and the melody work *together* to produce the desired sound. The idea of notes and chords all working together is called **harmony**. In most music the notes in the melody and the notes in the background chords 'belong', or are 'in harmony' together because they all come from the same 'family'. We'll look at this in a moment - just remember for now that chords and melody tend to work together well when they are somehow *related* to each other.

If notes and chords are used together randomly, the result is usually uncomfortable to the ear and we'd probably say the music sounded 'out of tune'.

So, knowing how chords and melody relate to each other is kind of important, and that's exactly what we're going to look at next.

The Musical Alphabet

It might look like you can play loads of notes on the uke, but there are actually only **12**. Amazingly, all the songs and tunes we play come from just these 12 notes! They can be used in different sequences to make melodies. They can also be grouped together in different combinations to make chords.

Understand that these same 12 notes are just duplicated all over the uke fretboard. You can see this in detail in the fretboard diagram at the end of the book (**Appendix 1**) but for now, just be aware that these twelve notes are *all* we need to make music and that each one can be found in several different places on the neck of the ukulele.

Let's call these 12 notes the **musical alphabet**. The musical alphabet looks like this:

A   A#/B*b*   B   C   C#/D*b*   D   D#/E*b*   E   F   F#/G*b*   G   G#/A*b*

Notice how some notes have been given a '#' or '*b*' symbol. These are the 'sharp' (#) and 'flat' (*b*) notes. Each sharp/flat note has two possible names and can be described using either, depending on the situation.

<u>Scale Basics</u>

Any one of the twelve notes can be used as a starting point for building a set of notes, or a **scale**. The starting note is referred to as the **tonic** or **root** of this scale. The two most common scales are the **major scale** and the **natural minor scale**. Now, because there are 12 possible notes to start our scales from, it means that there are 12 possible major scales and 12 possible natural minor scales. Make sense?

All **major** scales use seven of the notes in the musical alphabet.

For example, the C major scale contains the following notes:

C D E F G A B

The D major scale contains:

D E F# G A B C#

As you can see, these two scales have some notes in common. However, no two major scales are *exactly* the same - each one uses a unique combination of seven notes.

The **natural minor** scales also contain seven notes. For example the G natural minor scale is:

G A B*b* C D E*b* F

Like major scales, no two natural minor scales are *exactly* the same, each one containing a unique combination of notes.

These two scales are important as they're the basic building blocks for all the songs you'll probably ever play!

An Introduction to Chord Families

By combining the seven notes in a major scale in various ways, we can build a set of **seven chords**. I like to think of this as a **chord family**. The chords in the chord family are all related to each other because they all come from the same major scale (called the '**parent scale**').

Here are the chords in the C major chord family. Play them to hear the sound you get:

Notice how we get a mixture of both major and minor chords in the chord family. There is also a diminished chord, but don't worry too much about that one for now.

The notes in the C major scale and the seven chords in the chord family can be collectively called a 'key'. To be more exact, we could call them the 'key of C major' because C major is both the parent scale and the source of the chord family. Think of a **major key** as a set of chords (the chord family) and a set of notes (the major scale) which belong together.

We can also build chord families from the natural minor scale. When we do this we get a **minor key**, so called because the parent scale is minor instead of major. Just like with major keys, there are 12 possible minor keys, each one with a chord family containing seven chords.

In summary, the notes in the 12 major scales can be used to create 12 major keys and the notes in the 12 natural minor scales can be used to create 12 minor keys. Each of these keys has a chord family containing 7 chords with which we can create the background chords or **harmony** to a melody.

'Uke-Friendly' Keys

We can play in any of these major or minor keys, but in practice, on the ukulele we don't need to know about all of them. This is because most of the popular ukulele repertoire uses only a few of these keys - the ones which work well and sound the best on the uke. We'll come to this in a while.

The really good news is that you *don't* need to know hundreds of chords to play in the popular uke keys. You see, the same chords keep cropping up all the time! You'll be seeing how this works in the next chapter.

Major and Minor - Learning to Hear the Difference

Chord families contain a mixture of **major** and **minor** chords, so it's important to be able to tell the difference between them. Let's look at this now.

Grab your uke and play the chords shown next. Play them a few times until you are sure you can hear the difference in the quality or *colour* of each chord.

Don't forget to download your audio tracks at: **headstockbooks.com/uke**

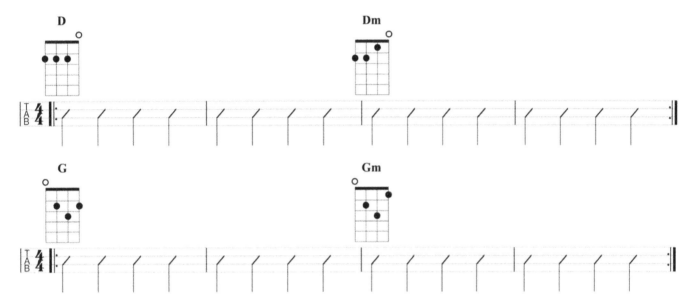

Now play these two chord sequences. Pay attention to the difference in the sound.

Example 1.1 (Audio Track 1.1)

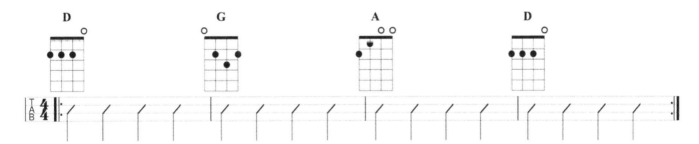

Example 1.2 (Audio Track 1.2)

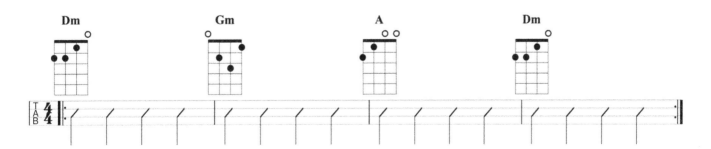

The first chord sequence uses **major** chords, giving a bright, happy sound and mood. The second sequence uses **minor** chords, giving a much darker, more sombre sound.

Play these exercises a few more times, listening *carefully* to the difference in sound between major and minor chords. This is a simple but important step for developing your listening powers as a musician.

Having compared the major and minor sounds, let's quickly look at the difference between the chords from a theoretical point of view.

Major and minor chords are actually only one note different. Look again at the D and Dm chords and notice which one it is. Do the same with G and Gm.

Try this Practical Exercise

Play the two chord pairs in the last example again.

Listen carefully to the second string with D and Dm pair and the first string with G and Gm pair. Hear the note changing to give you either the major or minor sound and colour?

Notice how it is only a difference of one note moving by one fret, or a *semitone* to use its technical name. This applies when we change from any major to minor chord starting from the same root note (E to Em, A to Am, Bb to Bbm etc.).

Stick with this exercise for a while, training yourself to hear the change clearly. This may seem simple, but it's a great way to start building your listening skills.

Congratulations, you've completed the first chapter!

We've covered some important concepts, so you might want to go through everything again to make sure that you understand it all. When you're ready, test yourself with the following quiz and check your answers to make sure you're on the right track.

Good luck, and when you're ready, move on to the next chapter where we'll look at chord families and see how incredibly useful they are.

See you then.

Quick Quiz

1. How many notes are there in the musical alphabet?

2. From the musical alphabet we can make how many major and minor keys?

3. The notes in a melody and the background chords should work together well. How could we describe this?

4. How many chords are there in a chord family?

5. Chord families mostly contain which two types of chord?

6. When you change from a major to a minor chord starting on the same root, how many notes change?

Check Your Answers

1. *The musical alphabet is made up of **12** notes.*

2. *There are **12** major keys and **12** minor keys.*

3. *When notes and chords 'fit' well together, we can describe them as being '**in harmony**' with each other.*

4. *A major or minor chord family contains **7** chords.*

5. *Chord families mostly use **major** and **minor** chords.*

6. *When a major chord becomes a minor chord only **one** note changes. The note in question changes by one semitone.*

Chapter 2: Chord Families

In the previous chapter we saw how there are 12 major and 12 minor keys, each one with its own family of 7 chords. This might seem like an awful lot of keys and chords to deal with, but don't panic because we're only going to look at the 'uke-friendly' keys. Later, you're also going to discover how the same chords can be used to make both major *and* minor chord families using a simple 'short cut'. This will make the process of learning about, understanding, and using keys a much easier task!

Ok, let's begin.

What is a Chord Family and Where Does It Come From?

Knowing which chords belong in a key's chord family is extremely useful. This is because the chord family for a key **tells you which chords can be used when playing in that key**. The chords in a chord family come from the notes in the **parent scale** of that key. The parent scale is the 'source' of the chord family.

For example:

- the chords in the **chord family** for the key of **D major** come from the notes in the **D major scale**

- the chords in the **chord family** for the key of **F major** come from the notes in the **F major scale**

- the chords in the **chord family** for the key of **A minor** come from the notes in the **A natural minor scale**

Hopefully this overview of keys and chord families makes sense. For a more detailed explanation on this topic see my ***Music Theory for Ukulele*** book.

Roman Numerals and Chord 'Quality'

We get different types or *quality* of chord in a chord family and each one is numbered for convenience with a Roman numeral. Understanding this is very helpful when you're a musician.

As an example, let's look at the chord family for the key of C major; this is a good place to begin because there are no sharps or flats to worry about.

The C major scale is:

C D E F G A B

The C major chord family contains 7 chords, each one built on one of the notes in the scale. The C major chord family is shown in the following diagram:

I	II	III	IV	V	VI	VII
C	Dm	Em	F	G	Am	Bdim

As you can see, some of these chords are **major** and some are **minor**. Each chord is identified by a **Roman numeral from I to VII** (1 to 7).

This process is **extremely important**, don't skip over it because it's one of the secrets to understanding the music you play and ultimately learning to jam with other musicians.

Let's examine the type, or quality of chords I-VII now. This is shown in the following table:

I	II	III	IV	V	VI	VII
MAJOR	MINOR	MINOR	MAJOR	MAJOR	MINOR	DIMINISHED

You can see that Chords **I**, **IV** and **V** (1,4,5) are **major** chords.

Chords **II**, **III** and **VI** (2,3,6) are **minor**. Chord **VII** is a **diminished** chord. Don't worry too much about this chord for now, you won't need it very often and we'll look at it again later.

Let's do a little exercise. Grab your uke and play the C major chord family using the following chord shapes:

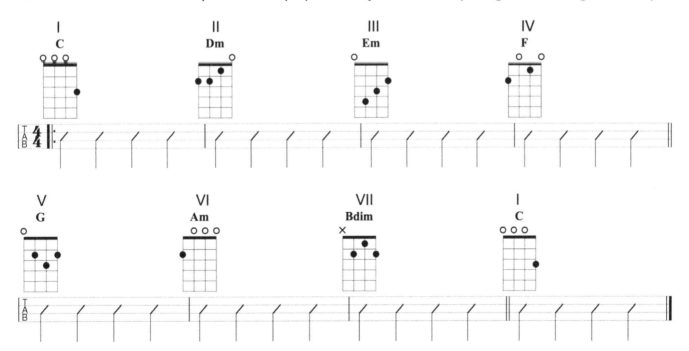

Slowly strum each chord once.

Listen carefully to the notes on the **3rd** string when you play chords I,II and III (C, Dm, Em).

Listen carefully to the notes on the **2nd** string when you play chords IV and V (F and G).

Listen carefully to the notes on the **1st** string when you play chords VI and VII (Am and Bdim) and the final I chord (C).

Those **individual notes** you hear moving along these strings are the notes in the parent **C major scale**. You can hear how the chords are **harmonising** with these. Each note of the scale is also the **root note** of the corresponding chord. Try this simple **ear training exercise**:

1. Listen to the sound of the C major scale as you play up the sequence of chords in the C major chord family
2. After several careful listens, try singing the sound of the scale as you play up the chords
3. Repeat!

Doing this simple exercise will really help you to relate the chords in the chord family to each other, as well as to the parent scale that they are derived from. So in summary, the chords in a chord family work together with the notes in the parent scale to create melodies and chord progressions which will sound 'in harmony' or 'correct' together.

This simple concept is how most music we hear is created.

Important: Chord Quality

Often people ask if it's ok to *change* the quality of the chords in a chord family. For example, could we change the II, III, VI and VII chords from minor to major chords?

Play the following example to hear what it sounds like if we do this:

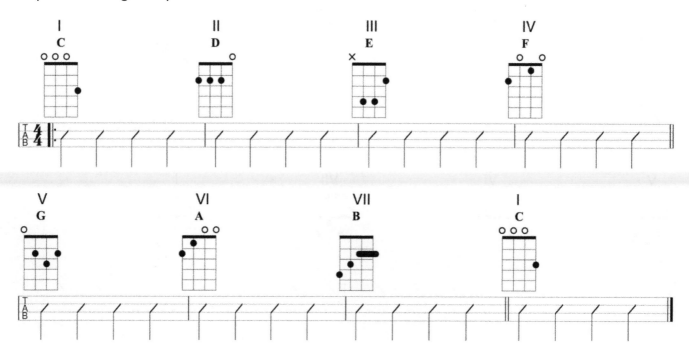

How does this sound to you?

To my ears, the chords don't blend or 'fit' together as smoothly as before. This is because when we change the quality of the chords in the family we are introducing notes which are *not* found in the parent scale. These foreign notes make the overall chord family sound different.

This doesn't mean we can *never* change the quality of a chord; songwriters often do this deliberately to create a 'surprise' sound in their song. For now though, we'll just stick with the standard chord qualities which occur in a major key chord family. Later in this book we'll examine how, when, and why you might want to change a chord's quality.

Chord Families for 'Uke-Friendly' Keys

The following table shows the chord families in the commonly used, 'uke-friendly' major keys of C, G, F, D and A (you can find a complete table showing *all* the major key chord families in **Appendix 2** at the back of the book):

I	II	III	IV	V	VI	VII
C	Dm	Em	F	G	Am	Bdim
G	Am	Bm	C	D	Em	F#dim
F	Gm	Am	B*b*	C	Dm	Edim
D	Em	F#m	G	A	Bm	C#dim
A	Bm	C#m	D	E	F#m	G#dim

Take a close look at each family and you'll notice that the quality of chords I-VII is exactly the same in each key:

I	II	III	IV	V	VI	VII
MAJOR	MINOR	MINOR	MAJOR	MAJOR	MINOR	DIMINISHED

Notice also that all the families apart from C major contain at least one sharp (#) or flat (*b*) chord. This is because their **parent scales** contain these same sharp or flat notes.

For example, the F major scale contains B*b*, so we get a B*b* chord in the F major chord family. You can actually work out the notes in each parent scale from the chart, simply look at the **root note** of each chord in a family.

Another important thing to notice is the overlap of chords in the different families. Some chords appear in several families, just in different numerical positions. Look through the table and find examples of this, then make a mental note of it for future reference.

Chords I and V

Let's try out some common chord sequences now and give them a 'label' we can use to help us understand them.

The first one is very simple and uses only two chords: **I** and **V**.

We'll start in the key of C major. Look at the chords in the C major chord family and you'll see that the chords I and V are C (I) and G (V). Grab your uke and play the following example:

Example 2.1 (Audio Track 2.1)

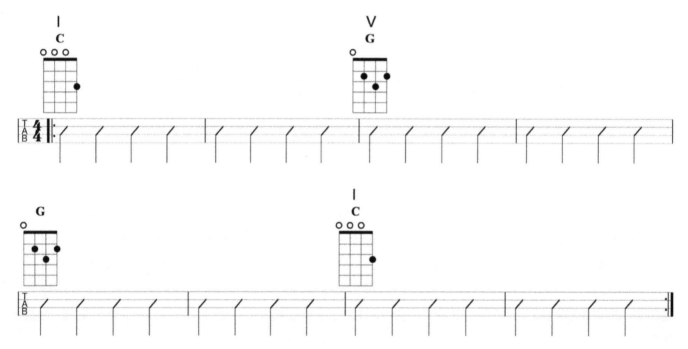

This is a **I-V-I** chord progression. Play it round a few times to hear the sound of the I and V chords when used together.

Now let's try it in the key of G using G (I) and D (V):

Example 2.2 (Audio Track 2.2)

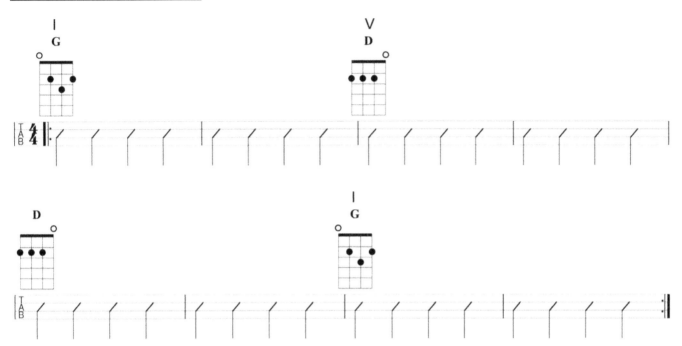

Try this Practical Exercise

Using the chord family chart, find chords I and V in a few different keys and play them together as well. As you do, listen carefully to the musical effect of the progression, noticing how it's similar no matter what key you play it in. It always sounds like a combination of chord I and chord V.

This chord progression may not be terribly exciting on its own, but it occurs over and over again in *thousands* of different songs, so it's important to learn to recognise it.

Listen to 'Jambalaya' by The Carpenters and 'Just One Time' by Mark Knopfler and Chet Atkins (you can find them online). Both songs are excellent examples of what can be done with two chords in a **I-V-I** progression. There are some great solos in both of these songs as well!

Introducing the IV Chord

Now we'll introduce the **IV** chord into the mix to get a **I-IV-V** progression. You can hear this chord pattern clearly in songs such as 'La Bamba' and 'Twist and Shout'.

The **I-IV-V** progression is very distinctive and is probably the most common chord sequence in popular music, forming the framework of thousands of well-known songs.

Grab your uke and play the following **I-IV-V** progression in the key of C major:

Example 2.3 (Audio Track 2.3)

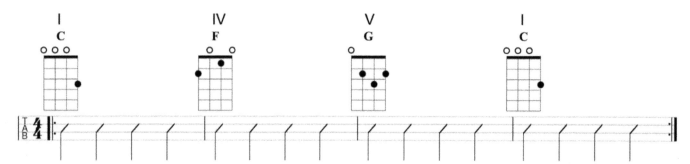

Remember, it's not just about playing the 'right chord shapes'; we're trying to train you to recognise all this stuff when you hear it! To do this, use the 'PLAY, LISTEN, HEAR' exercise I outlined earlier. It's a great idea to use this approach for *all* the musical examples in this book. You'll hear lots of different combinations of the I, IV and V chords used in the songs you play. The following progression goes **I-IV-V-IV-I** in the key of F major. Play it to hear the sound it gives us:

Example 2.4 (Audio Track 2.4)

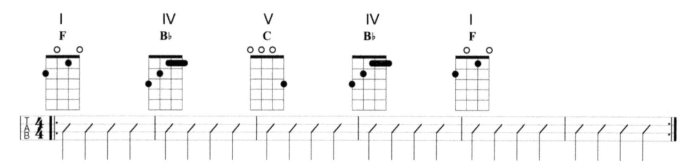

<u>**Try This Practical Exercise**</u>

Pick some other keys from the chord family chart shown a moment ago. Then work out how to play a I-IV-V-I and I-IV-V-IV-I chord progression in those keys. As you play them, *listen* carefully to the chord changes.

Make sure you do these exercises; it is only by **working with and experimenting** with everything in this book that it will become second nature and help you grow as a musician and ukulele player.

That's all for this chapter...

Hopefully you now understand the principle of using chord families to form common chord progressions and how to use Roman numerals to describe them.

We'll be looking at many other common chord progressions as we go through this book, and we'll be talking about chord families and Roman numerals a lot. For this reason, make sure you really understand *everything* in this chapter before moving on. I can't over-stress how knowing about things like keys, chord families, and I-IV-V chord progressions will help you on your ukulele journey!

Remember to test yourself with the following questions to make sure you have nailed everything in this lesson, and when you're ready I'll see you in the next chapter for more on chord progressions.

Quick Quiz

1. Where do the chords in a chord family come from?

2. The chord family in the key of G major comes from which scale?

3. In a major chord family, what quality are the I, IV and V chords?

4. In a major chord family, what quality are the II, III and VI chords?

5. In the key of C major, how could we describe a chord sequence which went C-F-G using Roman numerals?

Check Your Answers

1. *The chords in a chord family come from the **parent scale**.*

2. *In the key of G major the chord family comes from notes in the **G major scale** (the parent scale).*

3. *In a major key chord family, chords I IV and V are **major**.*

4. *In a major key chord family, chords II III and VI are **minor**.*

5. *In the key of C, the chord progression C-F-G is a **I-IV-V progression**.*

Chapter 3: More about Chord Progressions

In this chapter we'll look at what happens when we add the minor **II, III** and **VI** chords to our chord progressions.

First though, there's something I want you to understand...

A single chord progression does not *usually* make up an *entire* song. Sometimes this is the case, but more often a song is built using a series of simple chord progressions linked together. If it helps, think of chord progressions as being like the 'building blocks' of a complete song.

This is why the ability to recognise common chord progressions is so helpful - you can understand, learn and remember the songs you play much more easily. With practice you can learn to confidently play-along with other musicians, even if they're playing something you've *never* played before! In short, playing ukulele becomes much more fun as you increase your understanding and your listening skills.

With that said, let's continue our study of commonly used chord progressions as used in many of the songs we often play on the ukulele.

The 'Relative Minor' or VI Chord

Let's add the minor VI chord to some of the I-IV-V chord progressions we saw in the last chapter. Doing this gives us some of the most commonly used chord sequences ever.

Our first example is a **I-VI-IV-V** progression in the key of C major. Remember, use 'PLAY, LISTEN, HEAR' for all the examples in this chapter, including this one.

Example 3.1 (Audio Track 3.1)

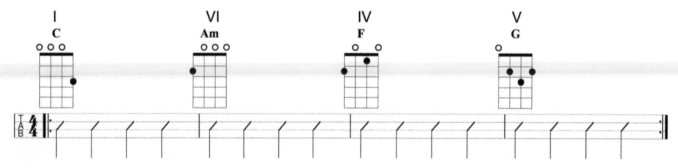

Listen carefully to the 1st string when you play C, the 4th string when you play Am, and the 2nd string with F and G. These notes are the **root notes** of these chords, and listening carefully to them will help you learn the sound of this chord progression.

Try this Practical Exercise

Now try the **I-VI-IV-V** progression in some other keys. Use the chord family chart from earlier to help find which chords to play. It might be a good idea to write the progression out, that way you won't have to keep checking the chart and can just concentrate on listening to the sound.

Also try listening to some of the individual strings as you play the chords, it will further help you get the feeling of this progression.

Maybe these progressions remind you of a song you play? If so, study the song and see if you can spot what's going on.

More on the Relative Minor Chord

The **VI** chord is sometimes called the **relative minor**. That's because it's very closely related to the **I** chord. To be exact, it's the **I** chord with the 6th note of the parent scale played instead of the 5th note which would normally be included in the **I** chord. Look at the following diagrams which show this happening with F and its relative minor, Dm.

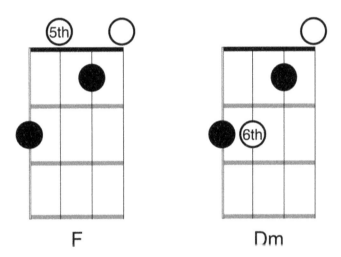

You can see something similar happening with A major and it's relative minor, F#m:

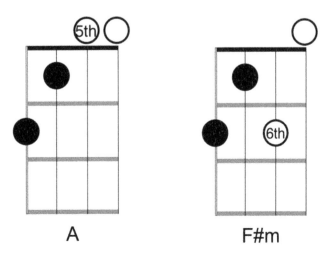

Play these pairs of chords a few times and listen carefully to the distinctive sound of I moving to VI.

Let's move on…

Quite often you will see the VI chord moving to the IV chord in a progression. This happens in the next example. Notice we're still using chords I, IV, V and VI, they're just in a different sequence. We can describe this progression as **I-V-VI-IV**:

Example 3.2 (Audio Track 3.2)

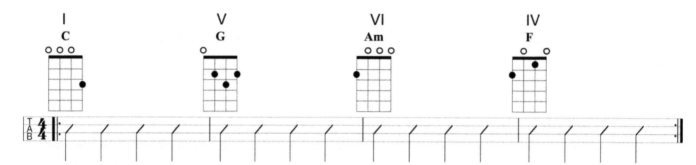

Here's the **I-V-VI-IV** progression again, this time in the key of A major:

Example 3.3 (Audio Track 3.3)

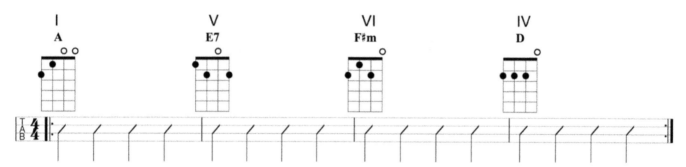

The **I-V-VI-IV** progression is very common in modern songs. Watch the 'Four Chord Song' by Axis of Awesome online. It might be hard to believe, but all the well-known songs in the video use this same simple chord progression!

Our next example is a song which uses **two** progressions made up from the same four chords. In both cases the VI chord goes to the V chord. The V chord, E, has been changed to E7 in this example - more coming on this soon.

The song is in the key of A major:

Example 3.4 (Audio Track 3.4)

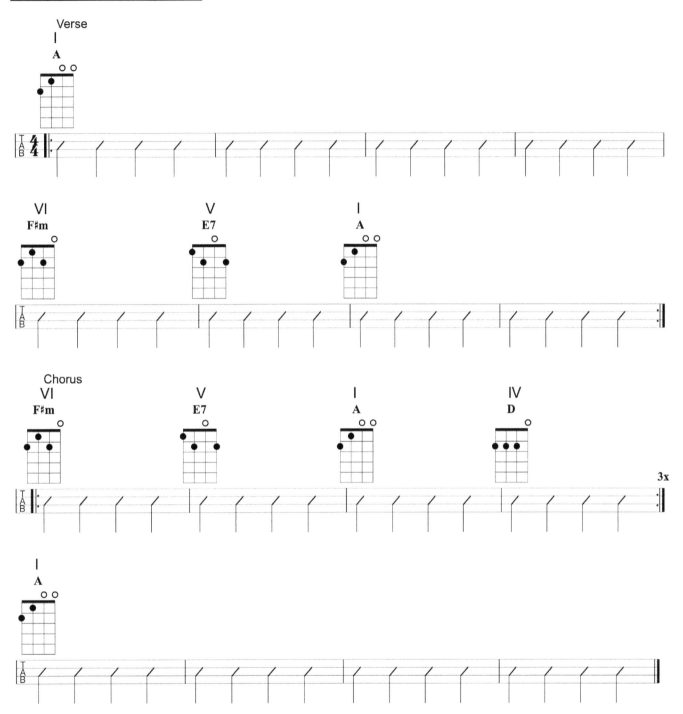

Let's analyse this song a little. The **verse** is simply a **I-VI-V-I** progression played twice. The **chorus** is a **VI-V-I-IV** progression played 3 times before returning to **I** for 4 bars.

Try this Practical Exercise

Practice playing the two progressions separately until you are comfortable with them, then put them together. Remember to use the 'PLAY, LISTEN, HEAR' approach as you do so!

When you're able to, play the song along with **Audio Track 3.4**. Get the chords firmly in mind and have a go at playing along without looking at the written chord sequences. Try to copy the rhythm and feel of the song too; rhythm is a *huge* part of making the songs you play sound great!

The II Chord

It's time to introduce another minor chord from the chord family into the mix: the **II** chord. Before we go any further, let's look at something interesting...

Go to the 'uke-friendly' chord families chart from earlier and look at the C major chord family.

Find the II chord, Dm, and the IV chord, F.

Now go to the F major chord family and find a Dm. You can see it is the VI chord or relative minor. As we've seen, this means it is very similar to the I chord in the key of F (which is F).

We can see how similar Dm and F are simply by looking at the common chord shapes used to play them which we saw a moment ago.

So, why does this matter? It means the two chords can 'replace' each other because they are so similar. For example, in the key of C we could use Dm (II) as a replacement for F (IV) because the two chords are so alike. We'll look at some examples now.

Let's use this as our 'starting' progression. The chords are going **I-IV-V-I-VI-IV-V** in the key of C:

Example 3.5 (Audio Track 3.5)

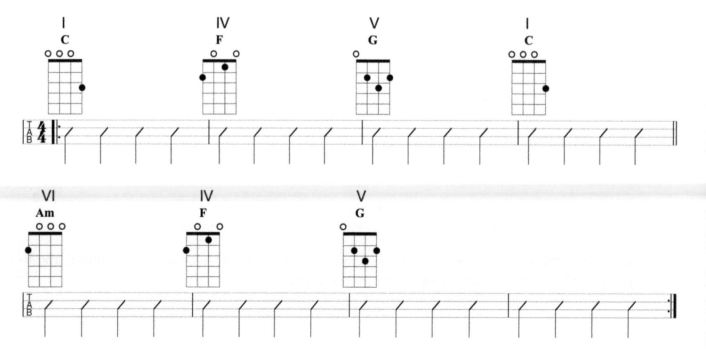

Now let's hear what happens when we use the II chord (Dm) as a substitute for IV (F). This gives us a **I-II-V-I-VI-II-V** progression:

Example 3.6 (Audio Track 3.6)

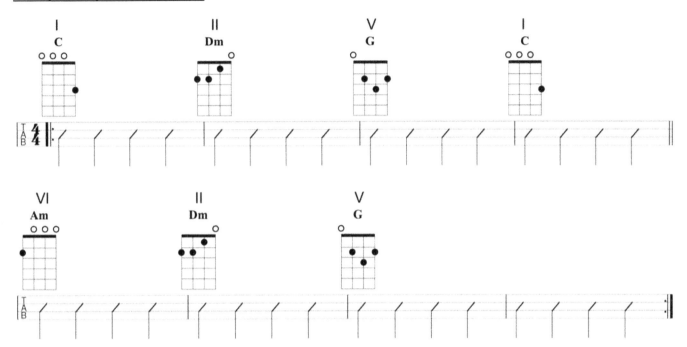

There's just a subtle shade of difference between the two progressions. Play them both multiple times to compare the sounds.

Now let's use II and IV in the same progression. This gives us yet another variation of the original 'starting' progression seen earlier in example 3.5.

Example 3.7 (Audio Track 3.7)

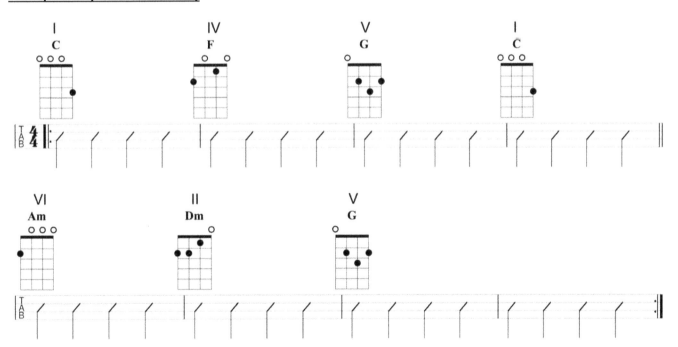

Notice the different 'mood' or 'flavour' each of these variations give us. Composers often use these different options to reflect the lyrics and express the desired emotion of their song.

This example also illustrates another really common application for the II chord...

See in the last example how the II chord is moving to the V chord and then the I chord?

This is known as a **II-V-I progression** and is extremely common in all music. Often the II chord is changed to a minor7 chord in a II-V-I progression to give a slightly different sound. The progression is essentially the same, it's just been 'decorated' slightly.

Now, I'm sure you don't need reminding of this, but everything we have said about the II chord applies to *every* major key.

Look at the next example in the key of F major. Check on your chord family chart from earlier, can you see what's happening in this chord progression?

Example 3.8 (Audio Track 3.8)

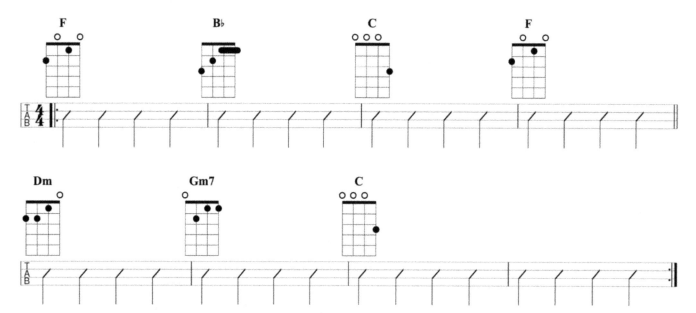

Note: I've used a Gm7 in this example instead of a normal Gm. This is just because it's such a great sounding chord!

✳ Try this Practical Exercise

You need to get used to playing and recognising the **II-V-I** progression, so using the chord key chart, practice playing the II-V-I sequence in some different keys. Remember to use the 'PLAY, LISTEN, HEAR' exercise from earlier to train your ear effectively.

The III Chord

Finally in this chapter we'll look at progressions using the minor **III** chord in the chord family.

This can be used in a **I-III-IV-I** to give a very distinctive chord progression.

This one always reminds me of 'Puff the Magic Dragon'! It's shown here in the key of C major:

Example 3.9 (Audio Track 3.9)

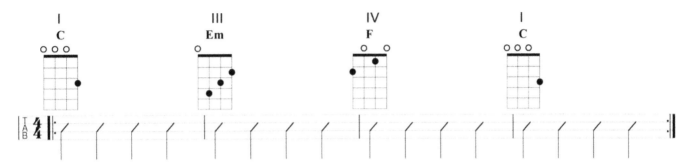

Try this Practical Exercise

Can you figure out how to play this progression in the keys of G, F and D? Try some other keys as well if you can play the required chord shapes.

Another common way the III chord is used is with the I and VI chords. This is shown in the following example in the key of G major:

Example 3.10 (Audio Track 3.10)

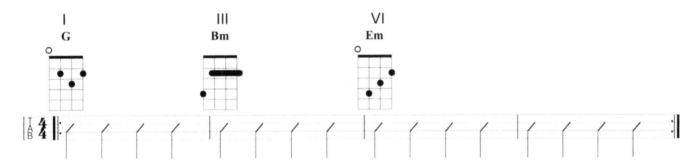

(Tip: listen for the descending 'run down' on the 2nd string for G and Bm, and the 3rd string for the Em)

Sometimes the III chord is used in a **I-II-III** progression. It will often continue up the scale, moving to IV or V (or both!). Play the following examples in C, F and G major to hear the resulting **I-II-III-IV-V** chord progressions.

Example 3.11 (Audio Track 3.11)

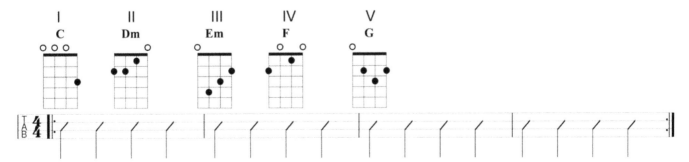

Example 3.12 (Audio Track 3.12)

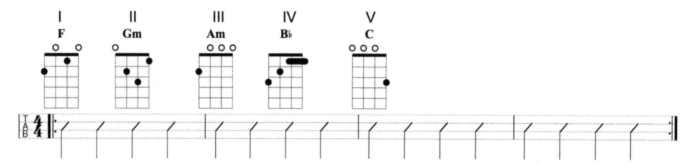

Example 3.13 (Audio Track 3.13)

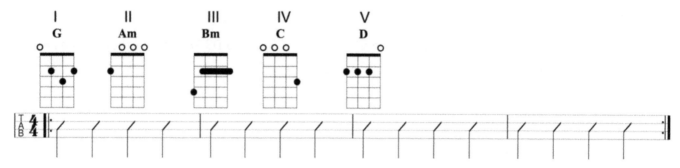

Try playing these progressions using the same rhythmic feel heard on the audio demonstration tracks. Play along with the audio tracks too when you can - it's a great way to practice.

As you play these examples, notice how you can hear the chords clearly moving up the scale in the **I-II-III-IV-V** progression. This is especially obvious if you listen to some of the individual strings as you strum the chords. Try it!

Combining Chords I-VI

So far we've used chords I-VI from the major chord family in various ways. We're going to look at the VII chord later on and you'll see that it plays an important part in our uke chord repertoire without us even realising it!

Let's leave this chapter with a chord arrangement that uses each of the chords I-VI. This arrangement uses the minor chords in a very recognisable way and is similar to a famous piece of music called *Canon in D Major* by Pachelbel. Although Pachelbel's composition was written in the late 17th century, the chord sequence it uses has been borrowed and used in some well-known songs in more recent times!

Try this Practical Exercise

Go through the following example and study the different chord movements. See if you can identify them. A good tip is to break the chord changes down, play them individually, and label them using the Roman numeral system.

Also see if you can recognise the minor and the major chords by their different *sound* qualities. This exercise will help you put together much of what we've done so far, so be patient if it takes a while. Just keep listening to and observing what you are playing... the results you want will come.

When you are ready, try jamming along to the track *without* the chords to guide you. Use your ears instead of the chord sheet!

Example 3.14 (Audio Track 3.14)

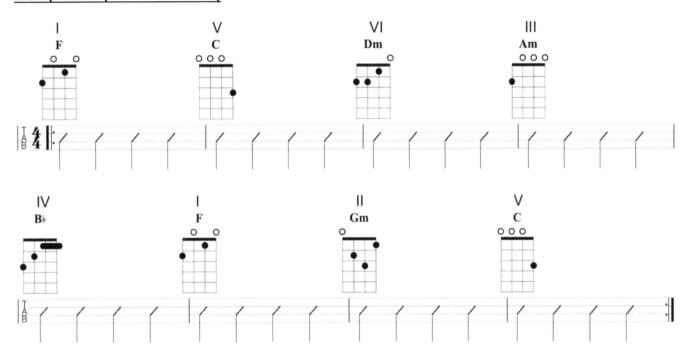

That's all for this chapter...

Congratulations, you've reached the end of **Chapter 3**.

Take your time with everything here, there are a lot of important concepts. Once you grasp them though, they have the potential to make an enormous difference to your musicianship and uke-playing skills, so keep at it!

In the next chapter we're going to look at the VII chord, both in its own right as a distinctive sound and as a major contributor to some of the most common and useful chords in popular music: Dominant7 chords.

So, go over this chapter as many times as you need to, test yourself with the following questions, and when you're ready I'll see you in **Chapter 4**.

Quick Quiz

1. Which chords in a major key chord family are minor?

2. The VI chord is also known by what name?

3. The VI chord is closely related to which other chord in the chord family?

4. The II chord in a key is sometimes used as a substitute or replacement for which other chord in the chord family?

5. The chord progression Dm-G-C in the key of C is what type of chord progression? Give your answer in Roman numerals!

Check Your Answers

1. *In a major key chord family, **II**, **III** and **VI** are minor.*

2. *The VI chord is also known as the **relative minor**.*

3. *The VI chord is closely related to the **I chord** in the chord family.*

4. *The II chord in a key is sometimes used as a substitute or replacement for chord **IV**.*

5. *The chord progression Dm-G-C in the key of C is a **II-V-I** chord sequence.*

Chapter 4: The VII Chord and the Dominant 7th

We haven't really talked about the VII chord in the chord family yet, simply because it isn't used as much as the other chords.

There are however some things you need to understand about chord VII, so we're going to get into this topic now. We're also going to look at another extremely important type of chord seen in virtually all music - the dominant chord.

Grab your uke and let's begin.

Chord VII and the 'Diminished Sound'

The VII chord is a *diminished* chord. 'Diminished' is simply a quality or 'type' of chord, just like major and minor are. Play the following diminished chord shape and listen to the sound.

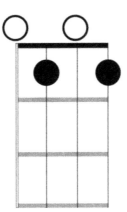

You'll probably agree, it has a tense, unsettled, and unstable sound – as if it wants to move somewhere! This desire to move is an important factor in how diminished chords are used, as we'll be seeing shortly.

If you look in any decent ukulele chord book you'll find there are several different ways to play a diminished chord, some requiring awkward stretches.

Luckily, there is an easy way to play *all* the diminished chords you'll ever need.

Here are the only two diminished chord shapes which you really need to know:

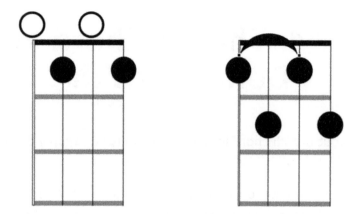

Now, technically these shapes give us a slightly *modified* diminished chord called a **'diminished 7th'**.

You don't need to worry too much about this, just know that these chords and the shapes used to play them often work well when playing the VII chord.

What's interesting about these diminished chord shapes is that **each shape can be used to play 4 diminished chords**!

In fact, any diminished chord we might need can be played within the first three frets on your uke.

Use this shape to play **B**, **D**, **F** and **A*b*/G#** diminished:

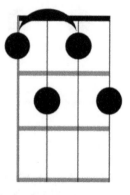

Use this shape to play **C**, **E*b*/D#**, **F#/G*b*** and **A** diminished:

And use this shape to play **D♭/C#**, **E**, **G** and **B♭/A#** diminished:

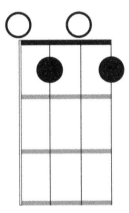

So, all in all, diminished chords are pretty strange creatures, but they're great for adding a distinctive, 'jazzy' twist to the songs we play.

Using the VII Chord

The diminished VII chord is most commonly found in 'jazzy' style ukulele songs like 'Over the Rainbow', 'Ain't Misbehavin' or 'Slow Boat to China'. Here are some typical chord progressions which use diminished chords. Listen to audio track **4.1** without playing along. Can you hear which chords are the diminished chords?

Check the following example to see if you were right, then play it to hear the sound the chords give us.

Example 4.1 (Audio Track 4.1)

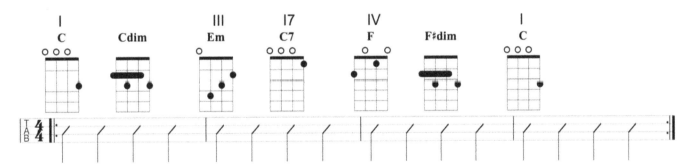

Very often the diminished chord is providing a harmony to a melody line moving in half-steps or semitones like in the following exercise. You can hear the melody moving in semitones along the C string.

Example 4.2 (Audio Track 4.2)

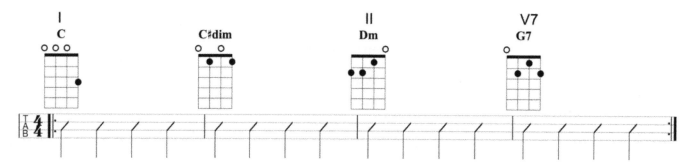

Diminished and Dominant7 Chords

There's a particular aspect of this VII diminished chord which gives us one of the most common and distinctive musical sounds there is. Grab your uke and play the following short chord sequence:

Note: Listen to what's happening on the 1st string as you play these two chords.

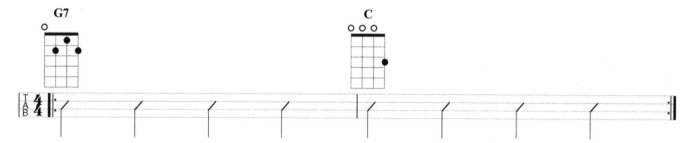

Can you hear how G7 'pulls' to go to C? We'll see why this is in a moment, but first, notice how the G7 chord contains the same 3 notes (B, D, F) found in Bdim, chord VII in the C major chord family.

The musical tension this creates is part of what makes the G7 'pull' towards C.

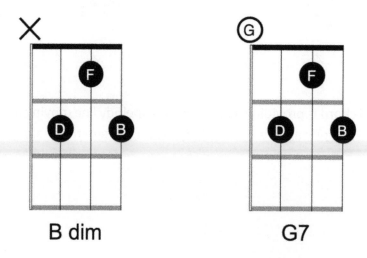

You may have spotted something interesting in these shapes - when we add a specific note to the VII diminished triad, we get a dominant 7 chord. In this case, we've taken the VII diminished chord (B diminished), added the root note of the V chord (G), and the result is a G7 chord.

The chord shapes we just looked at clearly show this happening.

So, hopefully you can see how we've created a new chord within the chord family simply by combining notes from the V chord and VII chord. The result: a V chord which has a dominant7 chord quality. This could be written as '**V7**'.

This doesn't just apply to G7 - *all* dominant7 chords contain a diminished triad. This is one of the reasons that dominant7 chords 'pull' to move somewhere else.

Try this Practical Exercise

Let's examine this idea in a different key. Play E7 followed by A. Notice how the E7 'pulls' towards the A (chord I). This is partly because the E7 shape contains the VII chord in the key of A (G# diminished). Again, the tension caused by the diminished sound in the E7 chord makes it want to move to the A chord.

Note: Listen to what's happening on the 4th string as you do this exercise!

Don't worry if you don't grasp *everything* about this diminished and dominant7 relationship yet. You *don't* need to be an expert on this to use both of these chords in the music you play, I'm just trying to take you a little deeper into *why* some of these chords sound the way they do and how they relate to each other within the chord family. I'm hoping this will encourage you to look for these kinds of things yourself, and get a deeper understanding of how music works as you do so.

Now that we've seen how the VII chord and the V7 chord are related, let's look at how we normally use dominant7 chords.

The 'Pull' of the Dominant7 Chord

As stated earlier, dominant7 chords tend to have a natural 'pull' towards certain other chords.

Normally a dominant7 chord is acting as chord **V** in the key we're in and is pulling to take us back to chord **I**. This can be described as a '**V-I**' progression, also known as a perfect cadence.

It's important to recognise the V-I movement from a jamming and ear training perspective because it's so common and helps us to understand where a chord progression is leading.

The next example shows a **I-IV-V7** progression in the key of C, with the V chord (G) being played as a dominant7 (V7) chord.

Example 4.3 (Audio Track 4.3)

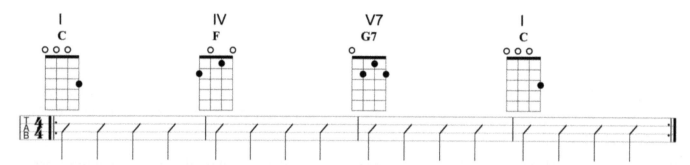

You don't *have* to play a V7 chord, a plain major V chord can work too. The following example uses them both. Listen for how the sense of 'pull' back to C increases when the G (V) changes to G7 (V7). This sets up the return to the I chord (C) when we repeat the progression.

Example 4.4 (Audio Track 4.4)

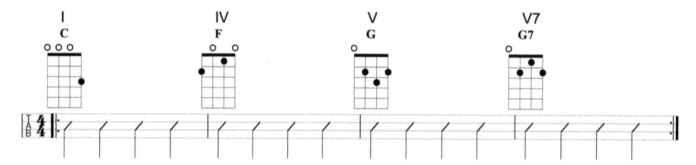

These are both straightforward chord sequences using I, IV and V chords with the V7 added for greater effect.

A lot of the time it doesn't matter whether you use a simple major V chord or its V7 version. In certain settings however, one option may work better than the other because it fits well with the melody being sung or played over the chords. Get used to trying both and listen for what sounds best to your ears.

The 'pull' that dominant chords create makes them great 'joining' chords. In other words, we can use them to 'pull' us smoothly from one chord to the next in a progression.

Play the following example in the key of G:

Example 4.5 (Audio Track 4.5)

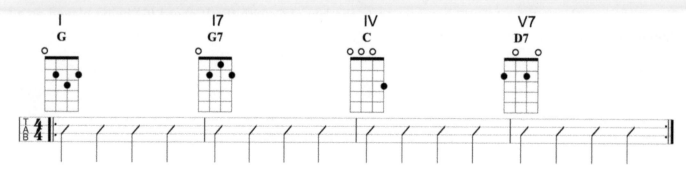

This is an example of how we can sometimes 'modify' the quality of a chord in the chord family and use it to do a particular job. The I chord (G) has been temporarily changed to G7. Hear how it pulls us smoothly into the C chord? That's precisely why we've changed it!

It works well because G7 to C is a **V-I** chord movement in the key of C. Check your chord families if you're not sure about this and you'll see what I mean. So, even though we're not in the key of C, we can 'borrow' the relationship between G and C in the key of C, and use it in the key of G to transition effectively between these chords. To put it another way, the I7 chord is 'setting up' the move to the IV chord.

When the I chord is changed to a dominant7 chord we can accurately describe it as '**I7**'. The progression you just played could therefore be described as **I-I7-IV-V7-I**.

These next three examples use the same idea in the keys of C, D and A. They're using a mix of V and V7 chords to help you learn to hear the difference.

Example 4.6 (Audio Track 4.6)

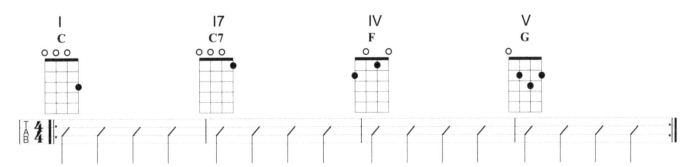

Example 4.7 (Audio Track 4.7)

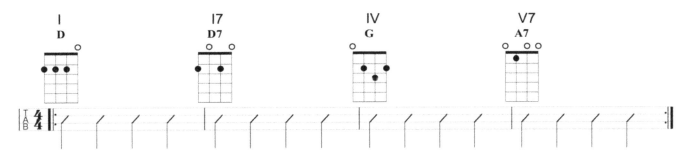

Example 4.8 (Audio Track 4.8)

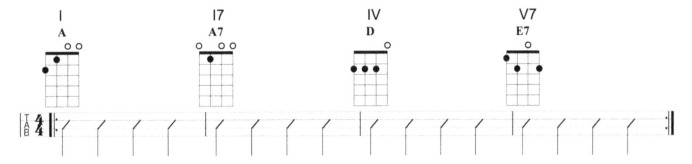

We'll be looking at the idea of changing some of the chords in a key to dominant7 chords in the next chapter of this book. For now, just become comfortable with the concept of using dominant7 chords to 'set up' the next chord in a progression; this is normally what we use them for.

Try this Practical Exercise

Play all the examples in this chapter using the 'PLAY, LISTEN, HEAR' approach we discussed in the intro to this book. As you play each one, listen out for the distinctive 'pull' of the V or V7 towards chord I, recognising this sound will help you a lot.

Also, try playing the V-I chord progression in a few different keys. Use both a major V chord as well as a V7 chord so you learn to hear the difference. If you need help finding the chords in some keys then see **Appendix 2** at the back of this book.

That's all for this chapter...

Now you know some of the sounds that we can get using the diminished and dominant7 chords. You're also familiar with how the V chord in a key 'pulls' to go back to the I chord, and how we can 'borrow' this sound and apply it to other chords in the key (for example with the I7 chord).

We'll be building on these ideas in the next chapter where we're going to look at some other great ways to use dominant 7 chords. So make sure you're comfortable with all the material in this chapter, test yourself with the following quiz questions, and when you're ready move on.

Quick Quiz

1. What kind of chord is chord VII in a key or chord family?

2. If we combine the VII chord with the root of the V chord in the key, what do we get?

3. Using Roman numerals, how could we describe a V chord which is played as a dominant7 chord?

4. We've seen how dominant7 chords have a natural 'pull' towards another chord in their chord family. Which chord do they tend to 'pull' towards?

5. C7 naturally pulls to which chord?

6. G7 naturally pulls to which chord?

7. D7 naturally pulls to which chord?

Check Your Answers

1. *The VII chord is a **diminished** chord.*

2. *When we combine the VII chord with the root of the V chord we get a **dominant 7** chord. This can be used as the V chord in the chord family.*

3. *When a V chord is played as dominant7 we can describe it as **V7**.*

4. *There is a natural pull effect between a **V7** chord and its **I** chord.*

5. *C7 would normally 'pull' to move to **F** (V-I in the key of F major).*

6. *G7 would normally 'pull' to move to **C** (V-I in the key of C major).*

7. *D7 would normally 'pull' to move to **G** (V-I in the key of G major).*

Chapter 5: Learning to Hear 'Stand-In' Chords

Back in **Chapter 2** we looked at using chords I to VII to harmonise a melody built using the notes in the parent major scale.

This approach explains how much of the music we hear is created, but it's not the complete picture! You see, sometimes the chords in a family are *changed* slightly to get a different sound, feel, or mood.

Remember this idea from the previous chapter, when we looked at changing the I chord into a dominant7 chord to get a smooth change to the next chord in a progression?

Well now we're going to examine this topic in more depth by looking at what I am going to call **'stand-in chords'**. You may see different terms used for the process I'm going to take you through, but I think stand-in is easy to remember and relates to our chord family in a way that is easy to see.

The actual theory behind stand-in chords can get a bit complicated, and we don't really need to go into *all* of it. I think it's more important for you to get a general idea of how the stand-in process operates, and most importantly, work at recognising the sounds it gives us.

So without further ado, let's begin our exploration of stand-in chords!

'Stand-In Chords': The General Idea

Here is the familiar structure of our major key chord family again:

I	II	III	IV	V	VI	VII
MAJOR	MINOR	MINOR	MAJOR	MAJOR	MINOR	DIMINISHED

Remember how the V chord can be played as a dominant7 chord as well as major? Well, it's the only dominant7 chord that occurs *naturally* in the key or chord family (this will make more sense in a second).

The stand-in process basically works by replacing the minor chords (II, III and VI) or the diminished chord (VII) with **major** or **dominant7** chords. We'll look at why we might do this in a moment, for now just accept it as an idea.

The C major chord family is shown below:

I	II	III	IV	V	VI	VII
C	Dm	Em	F	G	Am	Bdim

Using stand-in chords we could access some new sounds. The following table shows the C major chord family with chords II, III, VI and VII played as stand-in chords. Chord V is played as a dominant7 chord too:

I	II	III	IV	V	VI	VII
C	D7	E7	F	G7	A7	B7

Using Roman numerals for the stand-in chords, we could now describe the chord family as shown in the following table. Notice how the *same* Roman numeral is used with a '**7**' added, this tells us it has been changed into a dominant7 chord, and is standing in for the original chord:

I	II7	III7	IV	V7	VI7	VII7
C	D7	E7	F	G7	A7	B7

When we use a major stand-in chord instead of a dominant7, I'll use '**maj**' after the Roman numeral. So, you might see a label like **VImaj**, or **IIImaj**. Not all musicians do it this way, I'm using this method to make everything in this book easy to follow.

So that's the general principle of stand-in chords, but what kind of sounds do they give us?

<u>V-I Movement with Stand-In Chords</u>

It's pretty rare that *all* the stand-in chords in a key would feature in a single chord progression. Like anything, there are common situations where a stand-in chord will work well, and learning to recognise these is the primary aim. Let's hear what happens to the sound of a chord progression when we use stand-in chords as replacements for the chords in the chord family.

For each of these examples, remember to use the 'PLAY, LISTEN, HEAR' approach outlined at the start of this book. Over time your 'musical ear' will learn to label and recognise some of the common ways stand-in chords are used.

Play the following example in the key of C:

Example 5.1 (Audio Track 5.1)

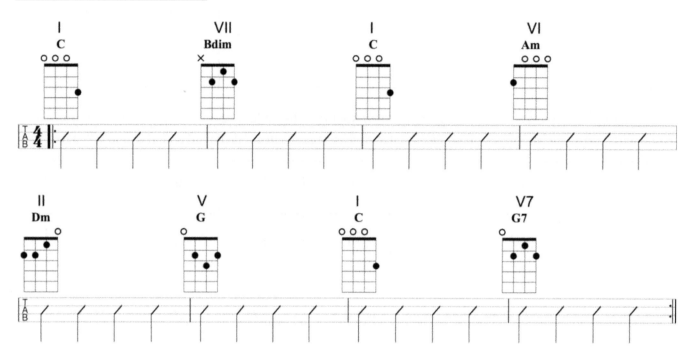

This example only uses chords which occur naturally in the C major chord family, but now let's hear what happens when chords VII, VI and II are changed to dominant7 stand-ins. Notice how the Roman numeral analysis changes too.

Example 5.2 (Audio Track 5.2)

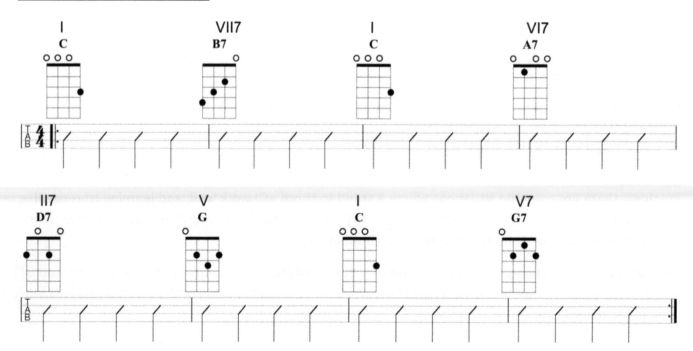

Hear what a difference this makes to the sound of the chord progression. The stand-in dominant7 chords give the chord sequence a really strong, vibrant sound.

What causes this?

There's a little bit of musical chemistry at work here. Remember from the last chapter how a V7 chord has a magnetic 'pull' towards its I chord? Well, take a look at the previous stand-in chord sequence and you should be able to see all the V-I movements within it:

- A7 to D7 (A7 is the V chord of D)

- D7 to G7 (D7 is the V chord of G)

- G7 to C (G7 is the V chord of C)

Check your chord family chart in **Chapter 2** and you'll see this for yourself. It's almost like we've looked for opportunities to use the strength of the V7-I chord movement and found a way to 'sneak' it into our chord progression!

Some songs rely completely on this cycle of V- I chord movements for their distinctive and memorable sound. Have a listen to this sequence in the key of G major:

Example 5.3 (Audio Track 5.3)

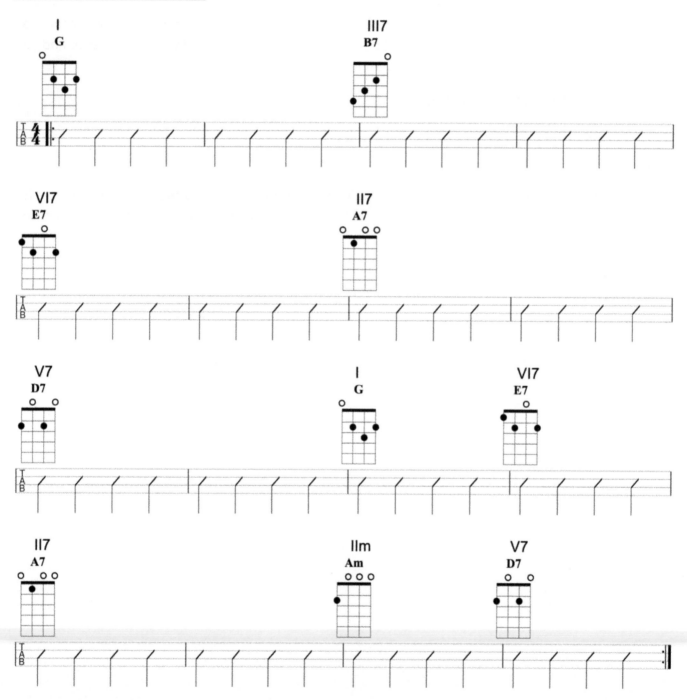

This progression uses a lot of stand-ins to create its distinctive sound, but notice how at the end of the sequence the II7 chord (A7) reverts back to the standard IIm (Am) chord. This creates some contrast and a change of mood in the sequence.

The examples we've seen so far may be using a lot of stand-in chords, but this isn't *always* the case. Often a progression will use them sparingly, it all depends on the sound the songwriter is after.

The III7 Stand-In

It's common to change chord III in the chord family into a major or dominant7 chord and use it to smoothly lead us into the IV chord. This creates a very distinctive sound which you can learn to recognise with practice. Play the following examples in the keys of G and C to hear the sound of the III7 stand-in chord:

Example 5.4 (Audio Track 5.4)

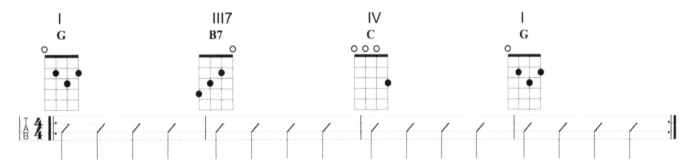

Example 5.5 (Audio Track 5.5)

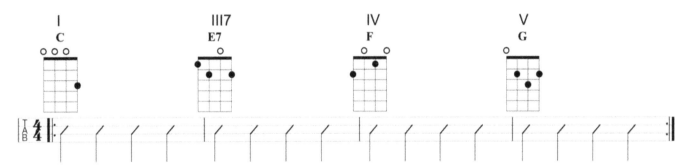

In both of these examples you can hear the III7 chord 'pulling' to move up a semitone (1 fret) to the IV chord. This common stand-in trick is heard in many well-known songs.

Try this Practical Exercise

This next example is similar to a song like 'A Fool Such As I'. It uses the I-III7-IV-I progression before moving to some other stand-in chords. Can you spot them?

Play the example along with the audio track when you're ready, and listen out for the sound the stand-in chords create.

Example 5.6 (Audio Track 5.6)

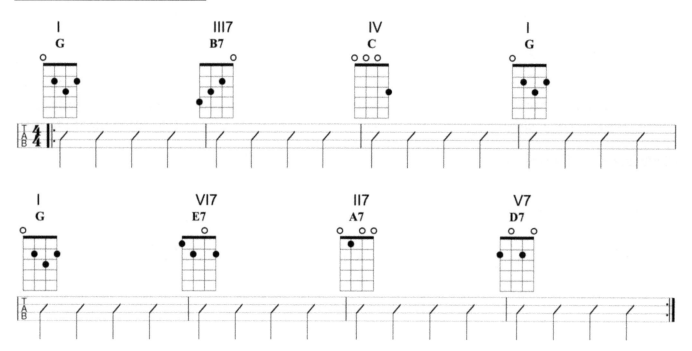

The Major II or 'Step Up' Chord

One of the most common uses of a stand-in major chord is with the II chord. This is a simple but effective variation which I call the 'step-up', or 'major step up'. I call it this because the stand-in chord is simply a major or dominant chord a whole step or a tone (2 frets) up from our I chord. From a more technical standpoint, we're simply changing the minor II chord into a major chord, and could therefore label it as **IImaj**.

In the key of C this would mean turning the Dm (II) into D major. Grab your uke and play the following example to hear the sound this creates.

The major II chord occurs in bar 6:

Example 5.7 (Audio Track 5.7)

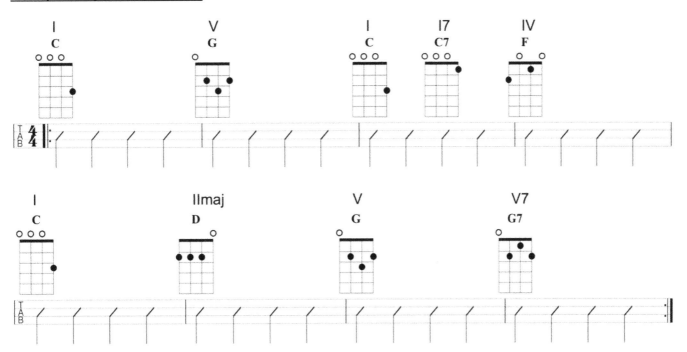

Hear how the D major 'step up' gives a slight, but distinctive, variation to this basic progression which uses mainly the I, IV and V chords in the key of C major.

Notice also how the major II chord (D) moves to the V chord (G and G7) before resolving back to I (C). This is an example of a II-V-I progression where the II chord has been changed from minor into a major chord (IIm is also often changed to dominant7).

This modified II-V-I is very common. It's worth learning and remembering this little trick, we hear it so much. Use the 'PLAY, LISTEN, HEAR' approach so that you begin to recognise the sound of it, this can help you figure out exactly where chords are moving to if you're jamming with other players.

Let's look at another common progression. Some of this example reminds me of 'All I Have To Do Is Dream' by the Everly Brothers. The progression is still in the key of C, but it begins on the IV chord (F). Towards the end of the sequence the 'step up' or major II chord appears again. As before, it's also forming part of a II-V-I progression which takes us back to C.

Example 5.8 (Audio Track 5.8)

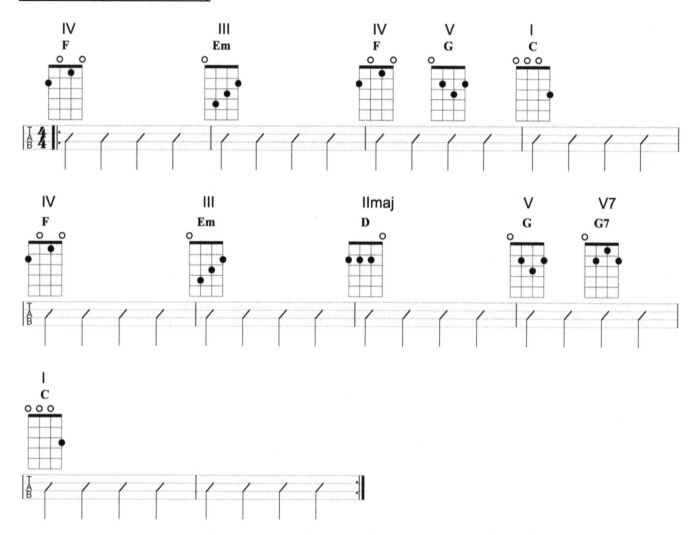

Listen to the dramatic contrast the major II chord creates after the Em to F chord change. It really gives the progression a 'lift'.

Two other things to note from this last example:

1. The step up effect is the use of the **IImaj** chord when playing in a major key. Although we're not moving *directly* from a C to a D chord in this example, the 'step up' sound is still heard because it takes place in the *context* of the key of C. Our ear is attuned to the key of C, so when we insert a D major chord we still hear the 'step up' effect

2. This example is used as a chorus for a song in the key of C, and as pointed out earlier, starts on the IV chord (F). This is very common and choruses in popular songs often start with the IV chord. Remember this, we'll be seeing it again in a later chapter

<u>Try This Practical Exercise</u>

Choose one of the 'uke-friendly' keys shown in the table in **Chapter 2**.

Play a **I-VI-II-V** chord progression in your chosen key. Play each chord for 2 bars to create an 8 bar chord sequence. Listen to the sound.

Then, experiment with using major or dominant7 **stand-in** chords for **VI** and **II**. Try different combinations of them, noticing how the sound changes.

Experiment with doing this in a few different keys!

That's all for this chapter...

Well done on reaching the end of this chapter. Hopefully you're starting to notice some results from using this book. Maybe you feel more confident when you play, you're beginning to spot what's actually happening in the songs you perform, or maybe you're even able to recognise some common sounds just using your ears? If so, then great! If not, don't worry; keep going and you'll soon see results.

Spend some time trying the different examples in this chapter and listening carefully to the sounds they give you. Also listen out for some of these sounds in the songs you perform on your own or in a uke group.

In the next chapter we're going to look at key changes, so test yourself with the following quiz questions, and when you're ready I'll see you in the next lesson.

<u>Quick Quiz</u>

1. What two types or 'qualities' of chord are commonly used as stand-in chords?

2. Which four chords in the chord family are most commonly replaced with 'stand-ins'? Answer with Roman numerals.

3. In the key of C, which chords would be used to play a I-VI7-II7-V7 chord progression?

4. What common chord movement are stand-in chords often used to create?

5. Where does a III7 chord often resolve to?

6. What do we do to make the 'step up' chord progression?

Check Your Answers

1. *Major* and *dominant7* chords are most commonly used as stand-in chords.

2. *The chords in the chord family most commonly replaced with 'stand-ins' are **II**, **III**, **VI** and **VII**.*

3. *In the key of C, a I-VI7-II7-V7 chord progression would be **C-A7-D7-G7**.*

4. *Stand-in chords are often used to create a **V-I** movement (or 'perfect cadence') within a chord progression.*

5. *The III7 chord often resolves to chord **IV**.*

6. *To make the 'step up' chord progression we use a **major or dominant7 chord** as a stand-in for the minor II chord. We could call these **IImaj** or **II7**.*

Chapter 6:
Key Changes and 'Modulation'

So far we've looked at progressions which use the chords in major chord families, perhaps with a few stand-in chords added for variation.

Sometimes to provide variety or drama, a composer will move away from the original key of the song and change into a completely new key. You'll sometimes hear this called *modulation*.

How a composer uses a key change will vary. Sometimes a key change may last for the remainder of the song, other times the song may revert back to the original key at some point. Sometimes it's debatable whether a song has really changed key at all, and the composer has really just used a few 'out of key' chords to create a different feel within a song.

There are lots of key change tricks you may come across, but it makes sense to study the most common ones first. That's the purpose of this chapter.

Finally, learning to hear and recognise key changes isn't always that easy, so don't feel discouraged if you struggle with some of what's in this chapter. Just play and listen to the examples using the 'PLAY, LISTEN, HEAR' approach we discussed earlier, and bit by bit things will get easier.

Ok, let's begin...

Simple Key Changes

Some of the most effective key changing techniques are also the simplest! The most common key change used in popular songs is probably when we move up by a **whole tone** and replicate the original chord sequences.

You can see this in the next example.

The sequence starts off in the key of C with a **I-IV-V-I-VI-II-V7-I** chord pattern.

Then in bar 8, the entire progression shifts up a tone from the key of C and is replicated in the key of D.

Example 6.1 (Audio Track 6.1)

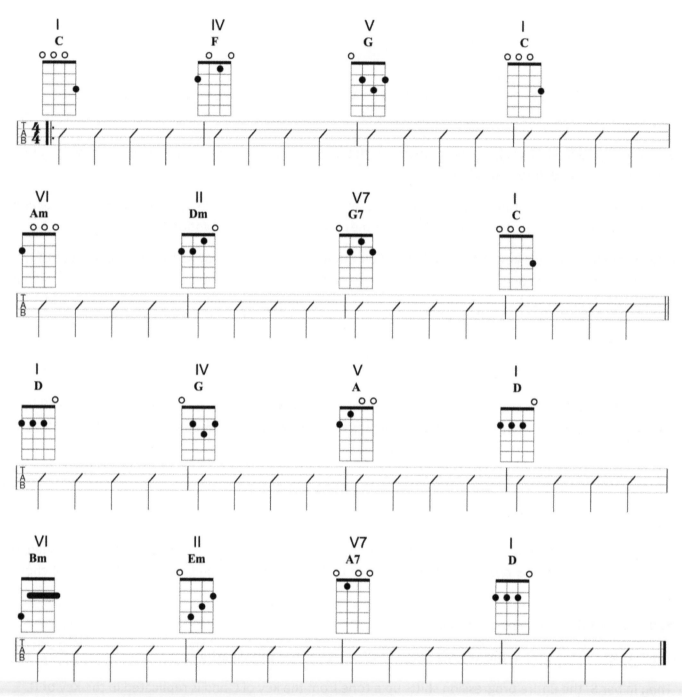

You can hear a perfect example of this in Kris Kristofferson's song 'Me and Bobby McGee'. Listen out for the key change at just under two minutes into the song. Can you hear it?

Sometimes a composer will change key by moving a chord progression up by a **semitone**.

If we applied this idea to the example you just played, the I-IV-V-I-VI-II-V-I progression in the key of C would move up a semitone into the key of C# or Db.

This produces a similar, dramatic 'shift' in the sound of the progression. Listen to Roger Miller's song 'King of the Road' to hear this idea.

Just over a minute into the song, the progression shifts up a semitone from the original key. Can you hear the effect this creates?

Try this Practical Exercise

Take 5 minutes to listen to the song examples I just gave you so you can hear these simple key change techniques at work!

Using the V Chord

In the examples we just looked at, there's no attempt to 'bridge' the key change with a joining chord to transition from one key to the other. Often this sounds good, but it's also very common to 'set up' or 'prepare' for a key change by using a chord which will lead you smoothly into the new key.

The most common way to do this is to use the **V chord** of the new key we're moving into. That's because of the 'magnetic pull' the V chord generates towards the new I chord. Let's look at an example of this now.

Play and listen to the following sequence. Remember to use the 'PLAY, LISTEN, HEAR' approach as you do so!

Example 6.2 (Audio Track 6.2)

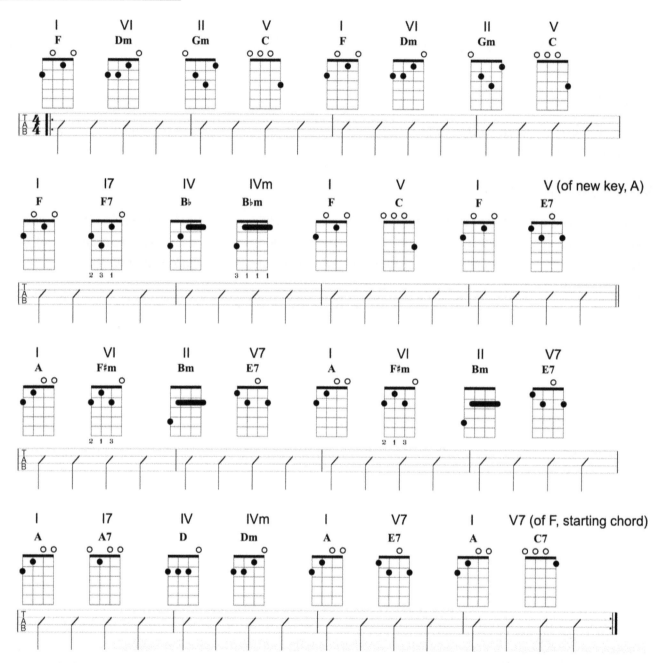

This example begins in the key of F major. In bar 17 it changes into the key of A major. Notice the E7 chord in bar 16, this is the V chord of A, and is used to 'pull' us smoothly into the A major chord and key change. The V chord is being used as a way to smoothly 'join' the two keys to create a more coherent chord progression.

At the end of the sequence the same technique is being used. This time we've inserted C7, the V chord of F major, to return us to the start of the progression.

This example you just played is similar in places to the old jazz standard 'Between the Devil and the Deep Blue Sea'. Try to find this song somewhere and have a listen to it.

Here's another example using the same technique. This time we're starting in the key of C, changing into the key of D, then returning back to the key of C again. For each key change, the V chord is used for a smooth transition:

Example 6.3 (Audio Track 6.3)

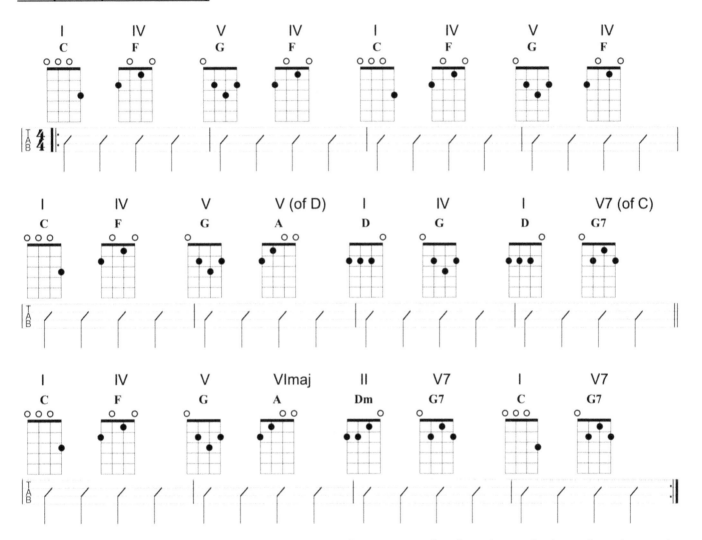

In bar 6 the A major chord is used to transition to the D major chord, and into the key of D. This works because A is chord V in the key of D major.

A few bars later, G7 is used to lead us to C, and back into the key of C major. This works because (you guessed it) G7 is the V chord of C major.

Note also the stand-in A major chord in bar 10. This is chord VI in the key of C, changed from minor into major. It works well because it 'pulls' us into the D minor chord that follows. This is because A (or A7) is the V chord of D minor too!

So you can see, V chords can be very useful when we want to transition smoothly into a new key. We simply use the V chord to 'set up' the change to the I chord in the new key.

Changing to the IV Chord Key Using Melodic Runs

It's very common to change to the key built off the IV chord. An example of this would be changing from the key of C into the key of F (F being the IV chord in the key of C).

Simple melodic runs can be very effective for transitioning into a new key. We can certainly change to the IV chord key *without* them, but a melodic run can 'lead' into the new key in a strong and logical-sounding way. They are particularly common and effective when we want to move to the key built off the IV chord in the key. Let's look at a few examples of this.

Listen to and play the following example. We start off in the key of C and play a typical I-VI-IV-V-I sequence.

In **bar 8**, strum the C chord once, then play the following run of notes:

C (open 3rd string), **D** (3rd string, 2nd fret), **E** (open 2nd string)

Note: this is written using tablature in bar 8 for readers who understand it. If you don't know how to read tablature, just use my verbal description to work out the note run.

These notes lead us up the first three notes in the C major scale (C, D, E) to F. This takes us into the new key, F, smoothly connecting us to the new I chord (F). Notice how the new key (F) is the IV chord of the starting key, C. Read this again so that it makes sense, then see if you can spot and hear all these things happening in the example as you listen and play it.

Example 6.4 (Audio Track 6.4)

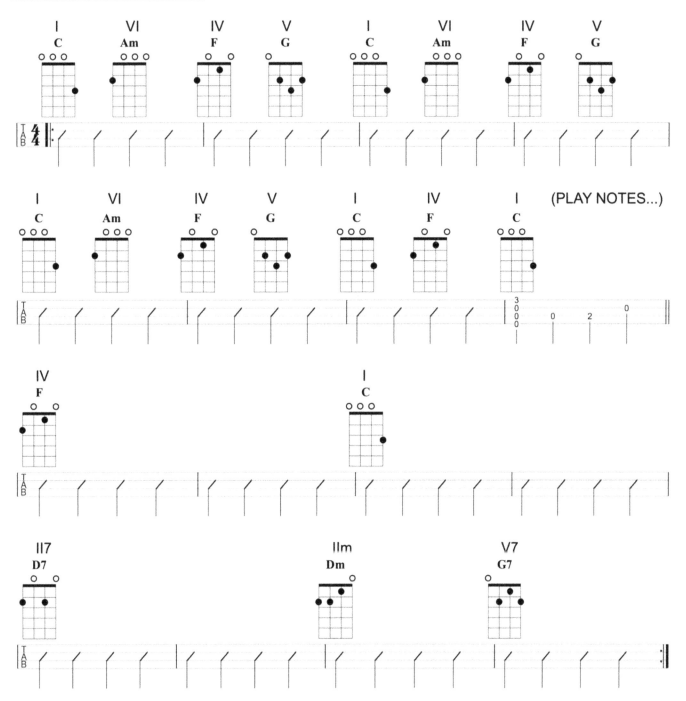

Let's look at how we could carry on this idea by changing from the key of F into the key of Bb. Play the following chord progression. In bar 8, strum the F chord once, then play a 3 note run going **A** (open 1st string), **Bb** (1st string, 1st fret), **C** (1st string, 3rd fret). This note run uses the 3rd, 4th and 5th notes in the F major scale and leads us smoothly to Bb, the I chord in the new key. Hear how this melody connects the two different keys.

Note: the connecting note run is written using tablature in bar 8. Use this if you can read tab, otherwise use my verbal description to work out the note run.

Example 6.5 (Audio Track 6.5)

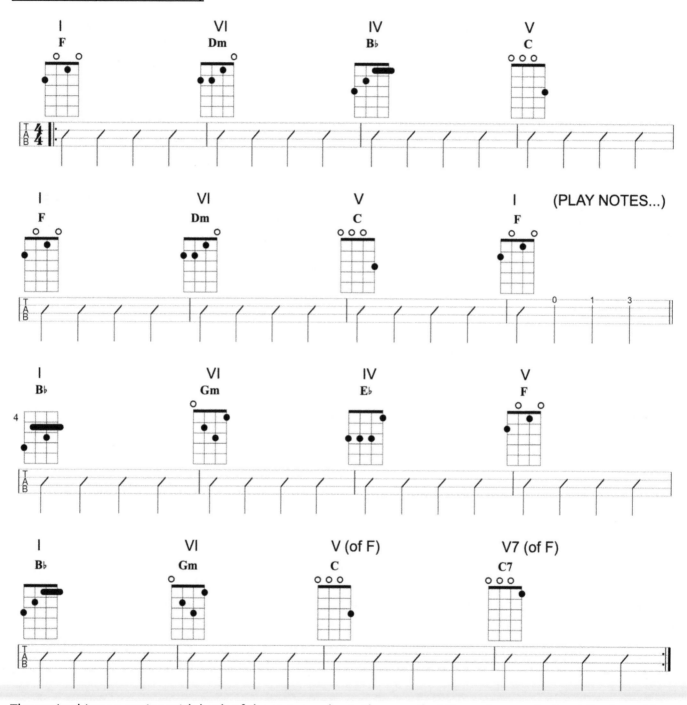

The main thing to notice with both of these examples is the way that the note runs 'set up' the transition into the key based around the IV chord. These are just two simple examples, but they illustrate the kind of thing we hear a lot during performances and on recordings. Often these kinds of 'connecting runs' will be played by the bass player in the band if there is one.

Listen out for these kinds of approaches - they can be very helpful because they normally make it quite obvious where the chords are heading to.

Changing to the V Chord Key

A key change to the key built off the V chord is also common. An example of this would be changing from the key of C into the key of G (G being the V chord in the key of C). The following example illustrates this approach. This might remind you of the well-known hymn 'All Things Bright and Beautiful'.

Example 6.6 (Audio Track 6.6)

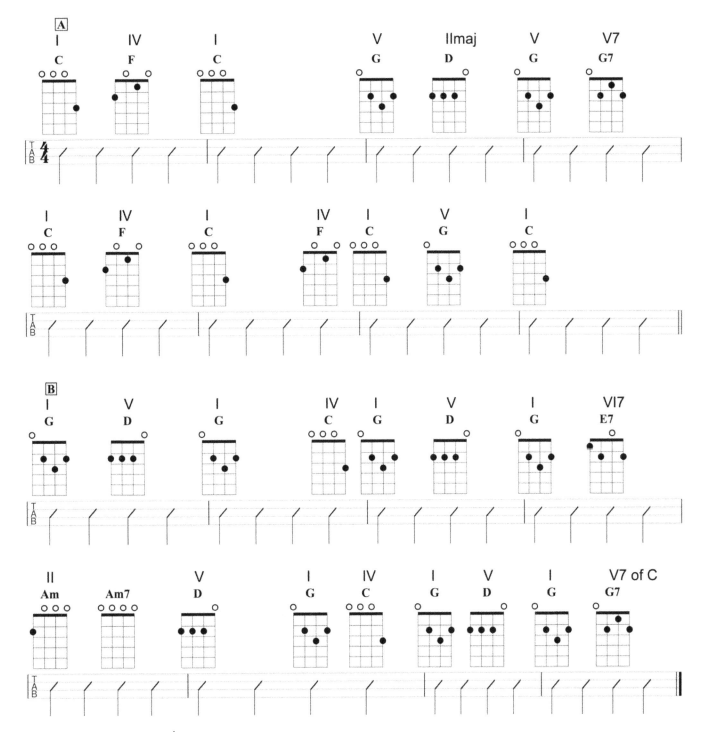

(Repeat A section again)

Looking at this example you can see that in each section of the tune the keys are using their own chord families.

In the key of C (A section) we are using only the I (C), IV(F) and V(G) chords from the C major chord family. When we change to the key of G in the B section we're using I(G), IV(C), V(D) and II (Am) from the G major chord family. The other chords, E7 and Am7, are added for interest and colour. Don't worry about them for now.

There doesn't appear to be a 'bridging' or connecting chord between the keys in this example. The reason the key change still sounds smooth is because the C major chord is in both keys (I in C and IV chord in G). The 'common ground' created by the C chord is being used to 'pivot' between the two keys smoothly. At the end of the example G7 (V7 of C) returns us to the key of C major.

Changing to the Relative Minor Key

We mentioned the **relative minor** in **Chapter 3**, but here's a brief reminder...

All major keys have a closely related minor key. This key is the minor key built on the **VI** chord in the major chord family. For example, the relative minor key of G major is Em because Em is the VI chord in the G major chord family.

Changing between relative major and minor keys is often used to give a marked contrast between different sections in a song, for example, between the verse and chorus.

One important and useful thing to remember is this:

The chords in any major key chord family are the same in the chord family for the relative minor key

For example, the relative minor key of F major is Dm. This means that the chord families for the keys of F major and D minor are exactly the same.

Let's look at two keys, C major and Am. These are relative major and minor and their chord families contain the same seven chords, as shown in the following tables.

I	II	III	IV	V	VI	VII
C	Dm	Em	F	G	Am	Bdim

I	II	III	IV	V	VI	VII
Am	Bdim	C	Dm	Em	F	G

Something important: notice how, even though the chords in both these families are the same, we've numbered them differently.

In the C major chord family, we're thinking of C as chord I.

When we think of these same chords as being in the key of A minor however, we think of Am as being chord I.

Let's look at an example of changing between these two related keys.

The verse to this song is in the key of A minor. This gives the music a sadder, more sombre, 'minor' mood.

In the chorus we change into the relative major key, C major. Notice how this changes the mood of the piece, giving it an uplifting, more optimistic flavour.

Example 6.7 (Audio Track 6.7)

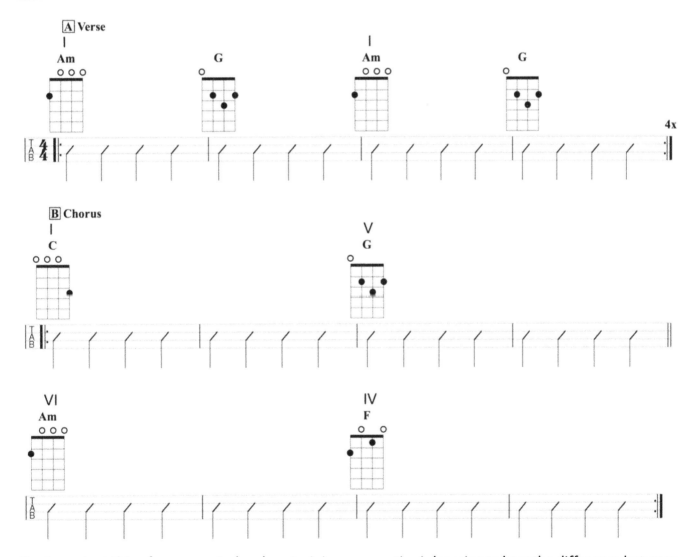

The important thing from a musical and ear training perspective is learning to hear the difference between the passages based around the **relative minor** chord sound and those based around the sound of the

major I chord. The change in the mood and feel of the song is unmistakable, and this is what we need to learn to recognise.

(By the way, that last example may remind you a little of the song 'Run' by Snow Patrol).

This next example also demonstrates the use of relative minor-led passages contrasting strongly with passages led by the major chords of the relative major key. Back in **Chapter 4**, I mentioned that the chorus or bridge part in a song often starts with the IV chord in a major key and that's what's happening here. The change to the major mood is led by the IV chord, then on to a V chord leading as you might expect to the I chord. We'll break this example up into sections for analysis.

The verse is clearly built around the relative minor chord (Am):

Example 6.8 (Audio Track 6.8)

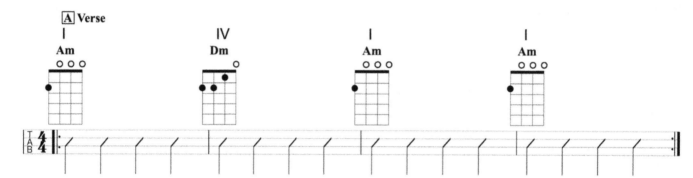

In the chorus we change into the major-led passage starting on the F, the IV chord in the relative major key, C. This is shown in the next extract:

Example 6.9 (Audio Track 6.9)

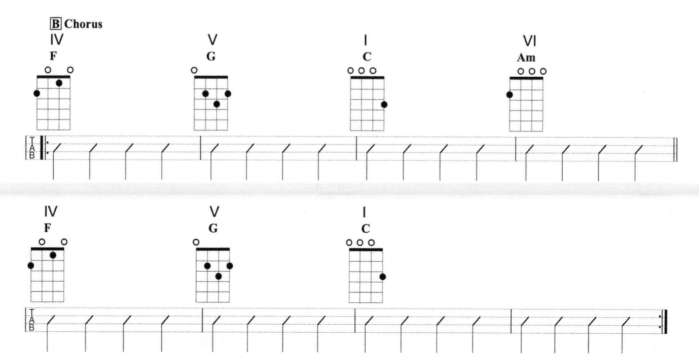

This major-led passage uses chords I, IV, V and VI.

Now have a listen to both of these joined together. This will highlight the contrast between the major and minor 'mood' of the two sections.

Example 6.10 (Audio Track 6.10)

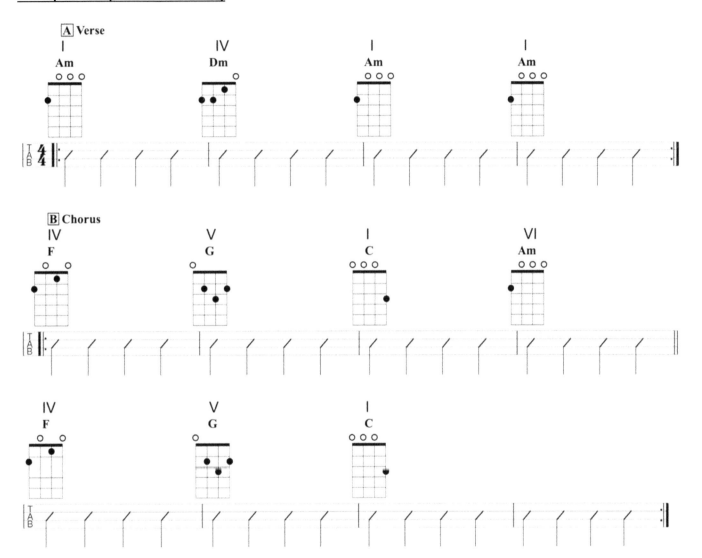

Relative and 'Parallel' Minor Keys

When a major and a minor key are based on the same note, we can describe them as being **parallel** keys. Examples of parallel major and minor keys would be:

- **C** major and **C** minor

- **G** major and **G** minor

- **E** major and **E** minor

Sometimes we *do* change from a major key to its parallel minor key or vice versa, but it doesn't happen that often.

Key changes between **relative** major and minor keys, like we've seen in the last few practical examples, are far more common in most of the music you're likely to play on your uke. This is just a little note to say this: don't get relative and parallel keys mixed up (lots of players do!) and make sure you understand relative major and minor keys, you'll see them both used together in lots of songs.

Try this Practical Exercise

Take the chord families for the keys of C major and A minor. Create a simple 8 bar chord sequence based around the C major I chord. This will sound like it's in the key of C major.

Now, shift the spotlight onto the Am chord. Treating it as chord I in the key of A minor, create a simple 8 bar chord sequence. This will sound like it's in the key of A minor.

Try playing them together. If necessary, tweak them to see if you can get a strong sounding chord change between the key of C major and its relative minor key, A minor.

Experiment, and have fun with this exercise!

Another Common Key Change

As I said earlier, there are many key changing 'tricks' used by songwriters and composers to create variety in their music. Some of these are quite complex, but in most of the uke repertoire they can be recognised and understood from what we have covered so far.

Before we leave the topic of key changes, let's look at one more technique which I call 'the step down' key change. This involves changing to the key a tone or whole-step (2 frets) *below* the original key. If you need a reminder on tones and whole-steps, refer to **Music Theory for Ukulele**, Chapter 2.

To get started with this kind of key change, grab your uke and play the following pairs of chords. In each pair, the second chord is a tone lower than the first chord.

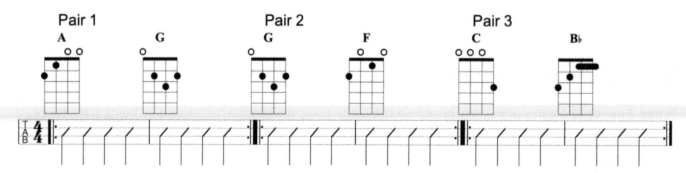

Ok, let's look at an example of a 'step down' key change.

The following song begins in the key of A before moving down a tone to the key of G.

Play and listen to it, then we'll analyse what's happening in more detail.

Example 6.11 (Audio Track 6.11)

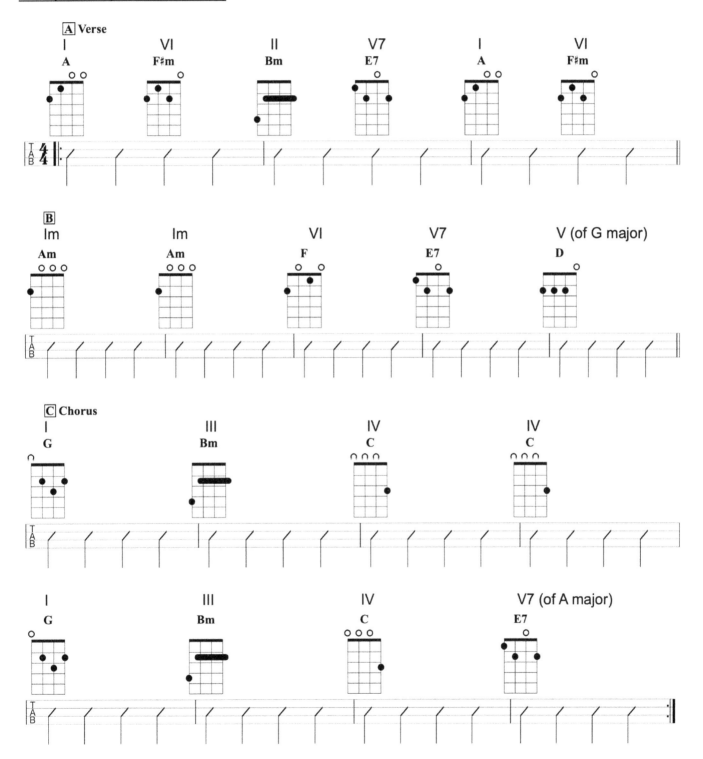

A section: This example begins in the key of A with a progression using the I, VI, II and V chords.

This is followed in the **B section** by a change into the parallel key of Am. The chords could be described as I (Am), VI (F) and V7 (E7) in this key. Next, we set up the change to the 'step down' key (G major) by introducing the D chord in bar 8. This is the V chord of G, and propels us nicely into the new key for the **C section**.

In the **C section** the progression is built with the I, III and IV chords from the G major chord family. Finally at the end of the example, E7 (the V chord of A) returns us to the key of A major again.

There's quite a lot going on in this example, so don't worry if it doesn't all make sense instantly. Read through the analysis again, play the example, listen to the sound and it will begin to become clear.

And if this example reminds you of something you've heard before, well it's using a very similar chord progression to 'Penny Lane' by The Beatles!

That's all for this chapter...

As I said at the start of the chapter, there are many ways to vary a song with key changes, and the approaches we have explored are just *some* of the more common techniques you'll see.

The main lesson to take away here is this: usually (not always) key changes don't have to be a mystery, and they don't have to block the way forward in learning a song. As we've seen, there's nearly always a pattern to them, and with a good working knowledge of the musical alphabet, chord families, and common chord progressions, it's normally possible to understand what's going on in a piece.

It would be less than honest of me to say that all this is easy - it does take time, practice and careful listening to become skilled at recognising different key changes. However, all we have covered so far in the book will get you on your way, and once you understand the principles involved you will have a better chance of recognising the various key changes you'll encounter.

In the next chapter we'll take a look at what are often called 'out of key' chords as well as some other common and identifiable chords songwriters use to create variation and attention-grabbing chord progressions for their songs.

So test yourself with the following quiz questions, and move along to the next chapter when you're ready.

Quick Quiz

These questions are all based on the following chord progression in the key of G:

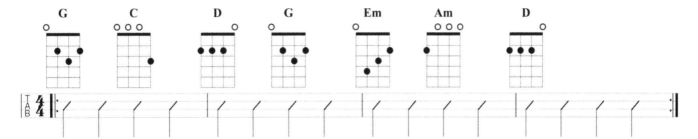

1. Replicate the chord progression using the whole step up chord change.

2. What chord would you use to make a good bridging or 'joining' chord from the original progression into your replicated version?

3. Why would this chord lead you strongly into your key change? Include a Roman numeral in your answer!

4. Imagine you wanted to move the **original** chord progression into the **relative minor** key. Which minor key would you change into?

5. How do you know this is the relative minor key? Explain your answer to check your understanding.

6. If you used a 'whole step down' key change on this progression, what would the chords be?

Check Your Answers

1. *A whole step up from G is A, so you'd replicate the chord sequence in the key of **A major**. It would look like this:*

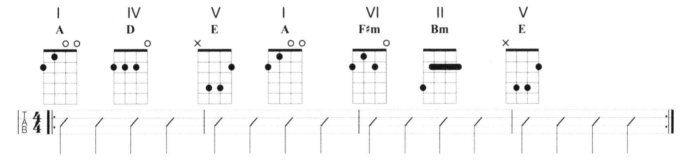

2. ***E7** would be the natural joining chord to change the key from G major to the key of A major.*

3. *E7 is a great 'joining' chord because it is the **V chord** in the key of A. It therefore has a 'magnetic pull' towards the I chord in the key of A.*

4. *The original progression is in the key of G. If you wanted to move into the relative minor key then you'd need to change into the key of **E minor** (Em is the relative minor of G).*

5. *We can tell Em is the relative minor because it is **chord VI** in the G major chord family.*

6. *Applying the 'whole step down' key change to the original progression in the key of G produces the following chord sequence in the key of **F major**:*

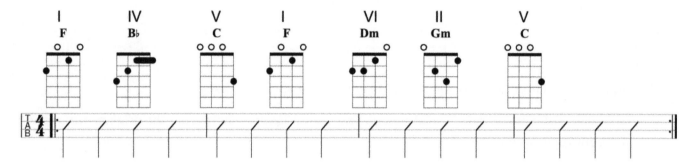

Chapter 7: Stepping Out of Key and 'Borrowed Chords'

Knowing about keys and chord families is a huge step towards being able to understand the music you play, but it's not the complete picture. This is because sometimes we encounter a chord or chords that *don't* belong in the chord family of the key a song is played in. These are often called 'out of key' chords, but I prefer to call them 'borrowed' chords because normally they've been 'borrowed' from the chord family of a closely related key.

In this chapter we're going to examine 'borrowed' chords. We'll see why they're used and look at the theory behind why they can work so well. As with everything in this book, make sure to play the examples and listen to the audio recordings. This way you'll train your ears to recognise some of these sounds when you hear them.

So grab your uke, and we'll get started.

Borrowed Chords and Stand-In Chords: What's the Difference?

I like to think of a borrowed chord as being slightly different to a stand-in chord. A stand-in is when we change one of the chords in the key to a different quality. In the key of C for example, we might change Em to E, or Am to A7. The roots of these chords are both in the C major chord family.

With a borrowed chord, it's different. Often we're introducing a completely new root and chord into the key, rather than just changing one of the chords in the chord family. As we'll see, this isn't always the case, but it's a good guideline to remember.

Commonly Used 'Borrowed' Chords

Let's start by examining some common ways that borrowed chords are used in the music we play.

The 'Tone Down' or *b*VII Borrowed Chord

Look at the following example in the key of C. It's using a borrowed B*b* major chord.

Example 7.1 (Audio Track 7.1)

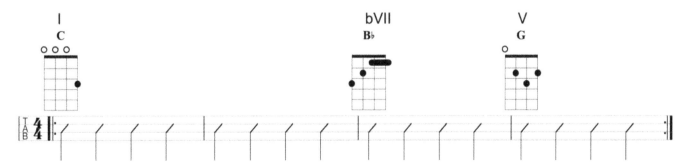

I'd think of the B♭ major chord as 'borrowed' because there is no B♭ chord of any kind in the C chord family. I hope you can see why I'm thinking of it differently.

In this particular case, the borrowed chord (B♭) is one tone down from the I chord of the key (C). This is a very common way to use a borrowed chord, and introduces a sudden striking change that really catches the listener's attention.

Here's another example of using a borrowed chord which is one tone below the root of the I chord. This time we're in the key of A major, so the I chord is A and the 'tone down' borrowed chord is G major. Grab your uke and play the example to hear the sound.

Example 7.2 (Audio Track 7.2)

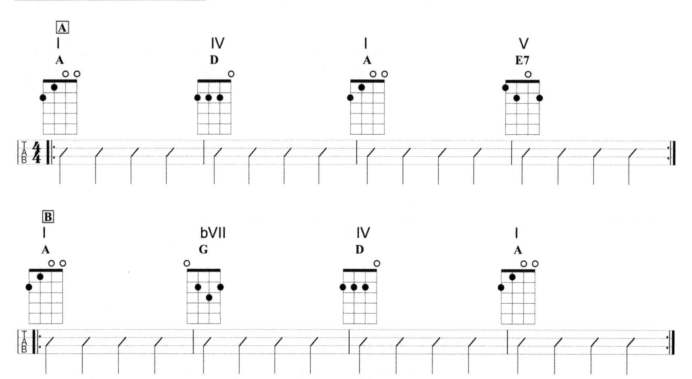

Let's look at this progression in a bit more detail.

The A section uses simple sequences of I, IV and V chords in the key of A. In the B section we're introducing the sound of the borrowed G chord. Notice how this gives the sequence a sudden 'lift'.

In the next example we can see the step down technique being used in a slightly different way.

Example 7.3 (Audio Track 7.3)

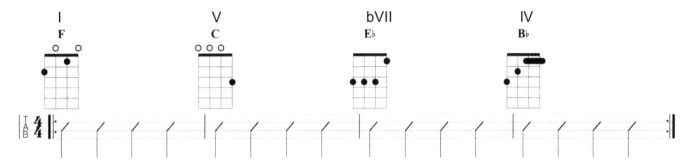

This example is in the key of F and using the I, IV and V chords (F, B*b* and C). The borrowed E*b* chord is a tone down from the I chord (F), and has been inserted between C and B*b*.

This also creates a series of I-V chord movements. This is because F to C is I to V in the key of F, and E*b* to B*b* is I to V in the key of E*b*. Don't get confused by this, just listen carefully and you should be able to hear a certain 'symmetry' between the two pairs of chords. If you can hear this symmetry, try to remember the sound it creates for future reference.

Here, the E*b* chord is the chord where we step out of key. I wouldn't really consider it a key change though, because the chords move back quickly into the key of F.

Why '*b*VII'?

Incidentally, if you're wondering why the borrowed chords have been labelled *b*VII in the examples, it's because we can think of this kind of borrowed chord as the *b*VII ('*flat seven*') chord in the key. Let's take a quick look at this.

The previous example is in the key of **F**. The **VII** chord in the key of F is normally E diminished. So, if the root of the VII chord is normally E, then it makes sense to describe a chord with an E*b* root note as the 'flat seven' chord (*b*VII). This is because the root is like the flattened 'version' of the VII chord. Make sense? We're playing the *b*VII chords as major chords here, as it's a common thing to do, but be aware that sometimes the quality might change. We don't need to go into too much detail on this, just try to understand where this *b*VII label comes from.

The 'Minor IV Chord'

Let's expand on the previous example by adding some other out of key chords. Grab your uke and play the following chord progression. Remember to listen to the audio track to help!

Example 7.4 (Audio Track 7.4)

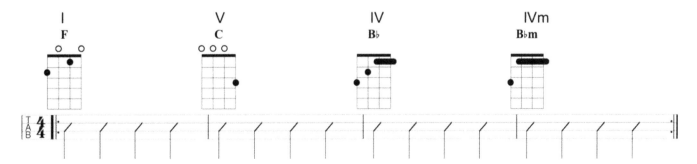

You probably noticed that this example uses another out of key chord: the Bb minor. This is basically chord IV in the key of F (Bb major) *changed* into a minor chord. We could therefore describe it as **IVm**. This is an instance of a borrowed chord whose root *is* present in the chord family and parent scale.

The sound of the IVm chord is very common, and with a little practice, quite easy to learn to recognise. We often hear the IVm used at the end of a chord sequence as shown in the next example. This time we're in the key of D major and the IVm chord is Gm. Use the Roman numeral analysis shown to help you see what's happening in this progression.

Example 7.5 (Audio Track 7.5)

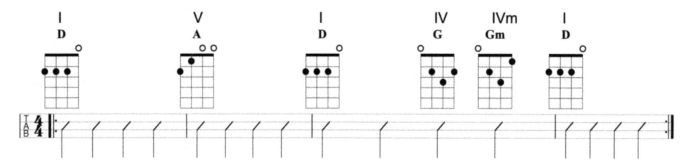

Example 7.6 (Audio Track 7.6)

Here's another example to try it's in the key of F. Use the Roman numerals to help you make sense of this progression too.

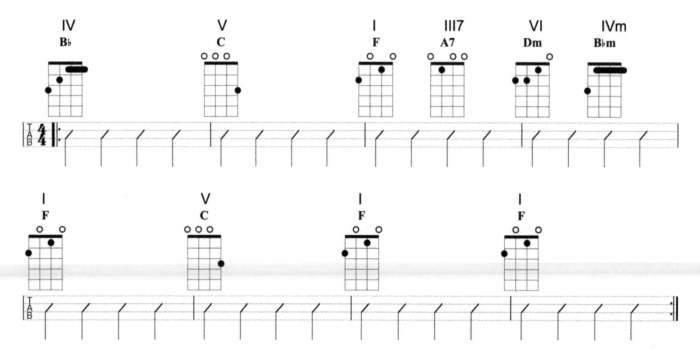

And that's the sound of the 'borrowed' IVm chord. Don't forget this simple chord trick, you'll hear it a lot!

Try this Practical Exercise

Choose a key and practice switching between chords I and IV. Do it over and over to absorb the sound.

Now, repeat the exercise but use the **IVm** chord instead. It will train you to identify this common borrowed chord when you hear it being used. Try the exercise in a few different keys.

The 'bVI Chord'

Another very distinctive out of key chord is the major 'flat six' chord, normally written as bVI. This chord can create a dramatic effect in a song, even if only used briefly.

First: what do we mean by **bVI**?

In the key of D, the VI chord is Bm. Move this down a semitone to Bb, play it as a major chord, and you get the **bVI** chord. Play the following to help this idea sink in and to hear the distinctive sound it gives.

Example 7.7 (Audio Track 7.7)

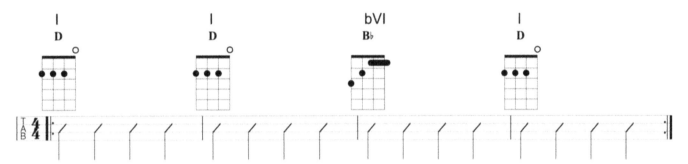

In the key of C, the VI chord is Am, making the bVI chord Ab. Play the following progression to hear the sound of the bVI chord again.

Example 7.8 (Audio Track 7.8)

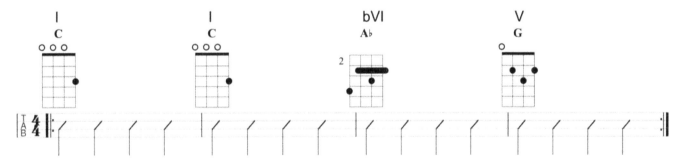

Here's a longer chord sequence using the bVI chord. This may remind you of the bridge section in 'Peggy Sue' by Buddy Holly.

Example 7.9 (Audio Track 7.9)

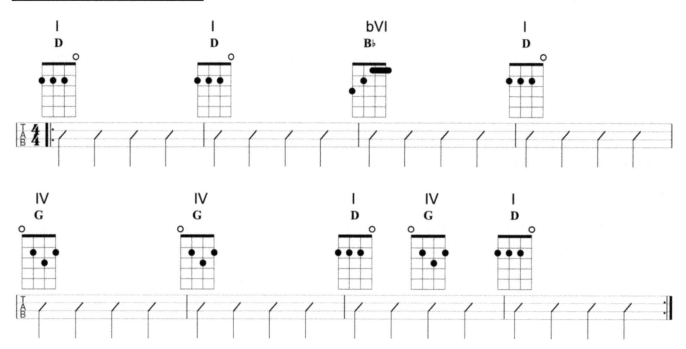

Hopefully you can hear the distinctive sound of the *b*VI chord, and what a powerful addition to simple I, IV, V chord progressions it can be.

Let's try a slightly longer example now.

This is in the key of D and uses the *b*VI chord combined with many of the other chord concepts we've examined so far.

It's also using some new techniques we haven't seen yet. Start by listening to and playing along with the audio track, then we'll analyse what's going on.

Example 7.10 (Audio Track 7.10)

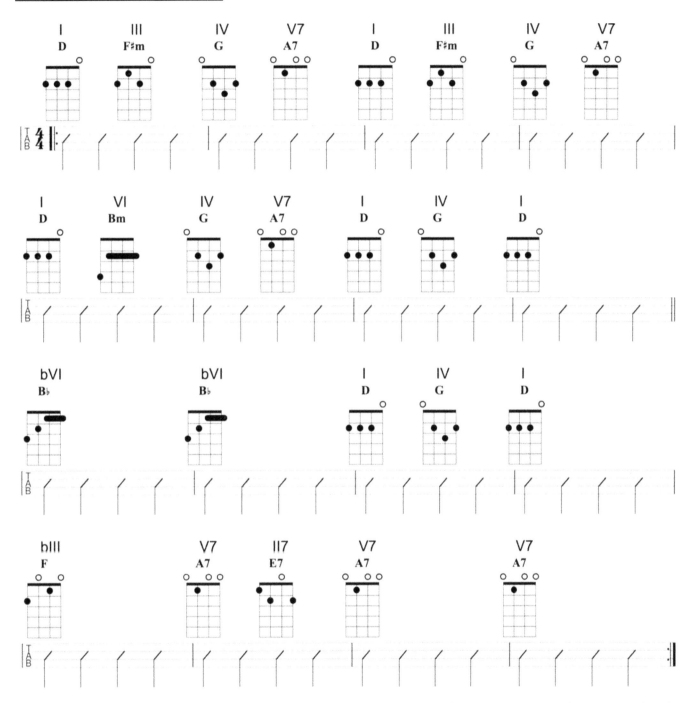

As you can see from the Roman numerals above the example, most of this progression is built using chords I, III, IV, V7 and VI from the D major chord family. There are also a few chords which don't belong in the chord family: B*b*, F and E7.

You should already be able to understand two of these borrowed chords: B*b* is the *b*VI chord, and E7 is a II7 stand-in chord, replacing the regular Em chord (II in the key of D major).

The F chord labelled as *b*III, well that's coming from somewhere else, and we'll be seeing where in a moment.

If you recognise the sound of this chord progression, then it could be because it's a bit like another one of Buddy Holly's songs: 'True Love Ways'.

Try this Practical Exercise

Take a key you're comfortable playing in, C or G major could be a good choice.

Using the chord family table in **Chapter 2** to help, compose a simple chord sequence using chords I, IV, V and VI.

Now experiment with some of the borrowed chord options we've discussed. Take some of the examples we've played with for ideas on how to use them. Just experiment, making a written or mental note of anything that works. Don't worry if some of what you play doesn't sound good to you - it's only through this kind of trial-and-error that you'll learn how to make it sound amazing!

Where do 'Borrowed' Chords Come From?

It might look as if borrowed chords are selected at random by the songwriter, but normally they're not. In fact, most of the time a borrowed chord is related in some way to the key and chord family a chord progression is in.

In many cases, borrowed chords come from the chord family of a **parallel** major or minor key.

So, what does this mean?

Major and minor keys are *parallel* when their **parent scales are built from the same root note**.

For example:

The keys of **G major** and **G minor** are **parallel** (both built on the note **G**).

The keys of **Bb major** and **Bb minor** are **parallel** (both built on the note **Bb**).

The keys of **D major** and **D minor** are **parallel** (both built on the note **D**).

Even though a parallel major and minor key are not *exactly* the same, they share enough in common that the chords in their chord families can be mixed together and still work. Of course, this needs to be done skilfully and tastefully to sound good!

The next table shows you the chords in the parallel keys of D major and D minor:

	I	II	III	IV	V	VI	VII
D major	D	Em	F#m	G	A	Bm	C#dim
D minor	Dm	Edim	F	Gm	Am	Bb	C

Let's refer back to **example 7.10** in the key of D major.

Perhaps now you can see where some of those borrowed chords are coming from?

The **b**VI chord (Bb) is related to the key of D major because it belongs in the *parallel* D minor chord family.

The **b**III chord (F) has been snuck in there too. It also comes from the parallel key. Both of these are highlighted in the following table:

D minor	Dm	Edim	F	Gm	Am	Bb	C

This parallel relationship is largely what makes the chords in **example 7.10** compatible with each other. If there was no relationship between them our ear might not accept them, they would simply sound jumbled and un-musical.

To make this point clear, play the following example to hear how a group of random, unrelated chords sound together:

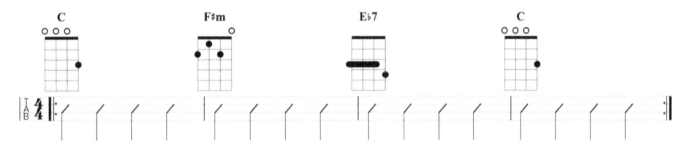

It doesn't sound all that great, does it? There's no compatibility between this set of chords to give a comfortable feeling to our ear when we hear this. The tendency for music to lean towards more 'comfortable' musical connections is why so many songs share so many common features. This is good news as it makes it that much easier to learn to recognise and play chord sequences simply using our ears.

By the way, if you look at the parallel minor key you'll see how the '**tone down**' chord we studied at the start of this chapter is in there too. In the parallel keys of D major and D minor discussed a moment ago, it's a C major chord. Can you spot it in the D minor chord family?

The concept of parallel keys explains why the 'tone-down' idea can work. It also explains why I referred to it as **b**VII in some of the earlier examples - it's the **b**VII chord in the parallel minor chord family. You don't really need to know all of this information by heart, it's just here in case you're interested in knowing more!

That's all for this lesson on borrowed or 'out of key' chords…

In summary, we can expect to see the key and chord family 'rules' we talked about earlier being stretched from time to time in order to create more interesting and engaging sounds. In many cases, any borrowed chords you encounter will be based on one of the concepts we've examined in this chapter. When you come across a chord which doesn't belong in the key chord family, pause and see if you can work out what kind of borrowed chord it is and why it's in the progression.

Is it a 'tone down' or **bVII** chord?

Is it a **II7** or **IImaj** chord standing in for the standard IIm?

Is it a **bVI** major chord?

Is it a **IVm** chord?

Is it borrowed from the parallel major or minor key?

Look out for all these devices being used in the songs you play. Remember also, you want to try and recognise what these borrowed chords sound like, so **play** all the examples I've given you and **listen** carefully to the sound of them.

With a little practice, common borrowed chords will begin to sound familiar when you hear them, even if you can't actually identify them to start with. Eventually, you'll find that your ability to recognise and identify them will also begin to develop.

This doesn't happen overnight, so be patient and stick with it. The important thing is to pay attention to what's going on in the music you play and try to look at what's beneath the surface instead of just blindly strumming the chord shapes! Do this, even just a little, and you'll see your ability grow.

That's all for this lesson, so test yourself using the questions given, and when you're ready I'll see you in the next chapter.

Quick Quiz

1. Look at the following chord sequence in the key of F. Which chord is the 'out of key' or 'borrowed' chord?

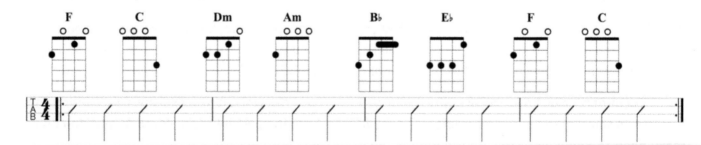

2. How could you describe the borrowed chord you identified in the previous question? I think there are two possible answers.

3. What do we mean by a **bVI** chord?

4. What is the **bVI** chord in the key of **D major**?

5. The following chord sequence is in the key of F major. How could you describe the **Bbm** chord? In what way does it relate to the key of F major?

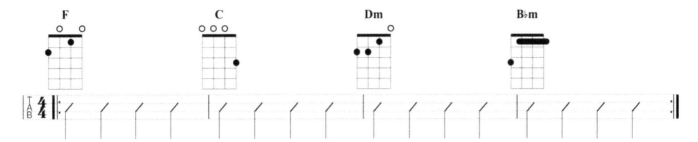

6. What is the parallel minor key of E*b* major?

Check Your Answers

1. *The out of key chord in the example is **Eb major**.*

2. *We could describe the Eb as a **'tone-down'** chord (i.e. one tone down from chord I). A more common label would be **bVII**. You could think of this chord as being borrowed from the parallel minor key of F minor.*

3. *The term bVI can be used to describe a chord **whose root is a semitone** down from the normal **VI** chord in a major key. The **bVI** is often played as a major chord. It too can be traced back to the parallel minor key.*

4. *In the key of D, the VI chord is Bm. The bVI chord is therefore **Bb major**.*

5. *Bb minor is not in the F major chord family. It's the minor version of the IV chord and would be described as **IVm**. It's related to the key of F major because it is the IV chord in the parallel key of F minor.*

6. *The parallel minor key of Eb major is **Eb minor**.*

Chapter 8: Spotting Song Formats

In this chapter we're going to look at some commonly used song formats and structures. This will make it easier for you to understand, remember, and follow the songs you play.

Now, you might be thinking:

Isn't the format of a song obvious? I mean, intro, verse, chorus, solo maybe, ending and outro possibly - what's so difficult about that?

Sometimes hearing the format of a song is obvious, but in my experience, many uke players can't always translate what they are hearing into playing terms.

For example, playing in a group, I've found that people often get completely lost during a solo or instrumental section, especially if it doesn't exactly follow the rhythmic pattern or the exact melody of the song. In this situation there is no 'syllable by syllable' guide on the song sheet lyrics to tell us when to change chords, instead we have to *feel* our way through the timing of the chord changes. Even if the chords are written out bar by bar, people still seem to get lost because they can't necessarily 'hear the song'.

Being able to recognise the format of a song can help you become more proficient at playing along with other ukulele players, so grab your uke, and prepare to explore some of the most common song formats you'll encounter.

The 12 Bar Blues

Let's take one of the most easily recognisable song formats to start with: the **12 Bar Blues**. This song format was used in the early rock 'n' roll songs, many of which were based on earlier songs of Afro-American heritage.

The 12 bar blues is 12 bars long and uses the **I**, **IV** and **V** chords in a set pattern. Grab your uke and we'll play a 12 bar blues in the key of A.

In the key of A:

A is chord **I**

D is chord **IV**

E is chord **V**

The chords are written out in the following example. See if you can play along with the audio track for this one!

Example 8.1 (Audio Track 8.1)

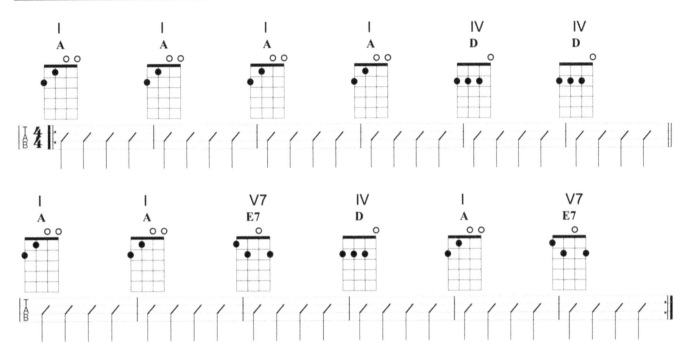

Let's analyse what's happening here. Use the Roman numerals written above the chords to help you understand this explanation.

Bars 1-8

We begin with 4 bars of A (I) followed by two bars of D (IV) then two more bars of A (I).

Bars 9-12

In bar 9 we go to our V chord E or E7 for one bar before moving down to the IV chord D for one bar.

In bar 11 we return to the I chord A for one bar.

In bar 12 the V chord (E or E7) is used to take us back to the start to repeat the form. A bit of 'blues speak' for you; this V chord is acting as the **turnaround**. This name is used to describe a chord or chord sequence which is 'turning around' the chord progression and setting up the repeat. This is the function of this final V chord in bar 12.

Try these Practical Exercises

Listen to the 12 bar blues using **audio track 8.1** and follow this analysis along.

Try to predict when the chords are going to change and listen for how the turnaround sets up the repeat. Just try to absorb the whole feel and sound of the 12 bar blues chord progression. With a little listening practice, your ears will get to know when the chords are going to change. This makes it *so much easier* to keep your place anytime you play a song based around the 12 bar blues (and a lot of songs are!).

It's also worth taking a listen to the original Elvis Presley recording of 'Hound Dog' to hear a simple 12 bar blues song. If you do, just note that in bar 12 there's a drum roll instead of a turnaround V chord.

Also listen to the way the guitar solo strays dramatically from the vocal line of the song both rhythmically and melodically, but the chord structure of the 12 bar blues stays the same - you can really hear this in the backing vocals throughout the solo.

12 Bar Blues Variations

Some songs use simple variations on the 12 bar blues format.

One variation is what is called a '**quick change**' blues. The only difference is that the IV chord is played in bar 2. This can nicely break up the sound of 4 whole bars on the I chord as in the previous example. Play the following quick change blues to hear the slight difference in sound. If you can, play along with the audio track.

Example 8.2 (Audio Track 8.2)

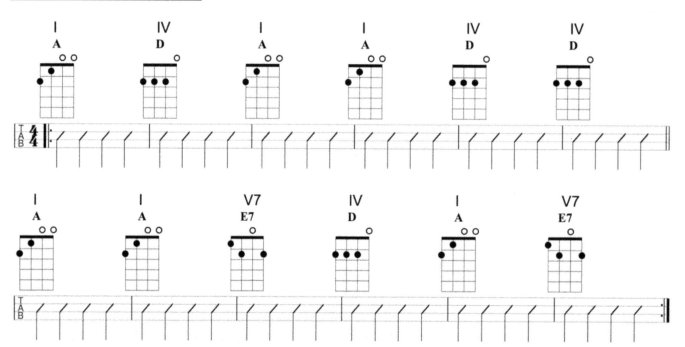

To hear a 'quick change' 12 bar blues listen to *Roll Over Beethoven* by Chuck Berry.

A less common 12 bar blues variation is shown in the following example. This is similar to the classic blues-based song 'Alberta'. Notice how we're using the V chord in bar 2. This example also uses a common I-IV-I-V turnaround in bars 11-12.

Example 8.3 (Audio Track 8.3)

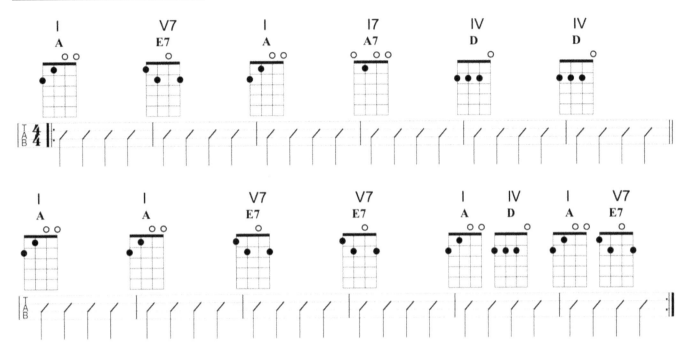

Hopefully you can see how the basic 12 bar blues format can be slightly changed to give a few possible variations. Listen to and play these examples, and you'll get to the stage where you can detect which version of the 12 bar blues is being used. You'll also be able to spot 12 bar blues forms when you see them written out as chord sequences in your uke songbook.

'Chord Riff' Songs

Another common song format is what I call the 'chord riff' song form. This is *my* name for a song which uses a short repetitive chord sequence played over and over. If you can spot how a song mainly uses the same chord sequence played round and round, it makes it easier to learn and remember.

Sometimes these songs will use a repetitive melodic phrase (also known as a 'riff') played over the repeating chord sequence. A good example is the classic rock song 'Sweet Home Alabama'.

The famous guitar riff it uses makes the song instantly recognisable, but it's still mainly based on a simple 4 bar chord sequence played over and over.

The chords are similar to the example shown next.

Example 8.4 (Audio Track 8.4)

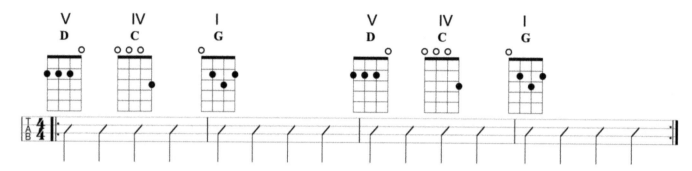

Play these chords along with the audio recording to practice them and become used to the idea of a short chord progression repeating over and over.

Play the following example. It's a simple 8 bar chord progression in the key of G:

Example 8.5 (Audio Track 8.5)

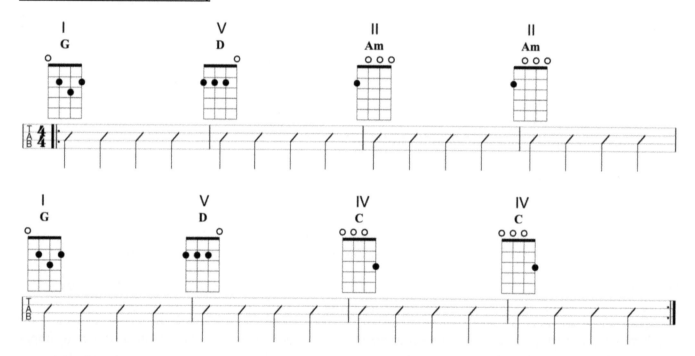

Sound familiar? This could be because it reminds you of 'Knockin' on Heaven's Door' by Bob Dylan. This is another example of a very famous song which is based on a simple repeating chord progression.

A couple of other songs which are based on a simple progression or 'chord riff' are Tom Petty's 'Free Fallin' and 'Learning to Fly'. Listen to them and see if you can hear what I'm talking about. Also look out for songs based on a 'chord riff' as you make music with other uke players.

'The IV Chord Chorus' Song

Let's look at a song format which I call the 'IV chord chorus song'. As with some of the other labels I've used to describe things, this is my own name for this idea - it's not a 'correct' musical term! The 'IV chord chorus' format creates a clear distinction between the verses and chorus of a song, making it easier to hear your way through it and know where you are at any time.

In the simplest form, the verse may be based on the I, IV and V chords, with the main emphasis probably on I. The I chord will commonly start and end the progression.

The chorus, however, will be led by the IV chord, giving a noticeable shift away from the I chord bias. Very often there is a **I7** chord linking the verse to the IV chord at the beginning of the chorus (we looked at this in **Chapter 4**).

Let's look at an example of this happening. Play the next progression in the key of G. Ideally, play it along with **audio track 8.6** if you can. Notice how the chorus 'breaks away' from the emphasis on the I chord by starting on chord IV.

This creates a 'shift' in the mood and colour of the song. Also notice the I7 chord at the end of the second line.

Listen to hear how it sets up the transition to the IV chord.

Example 8.6 (Audio Track 8.6)

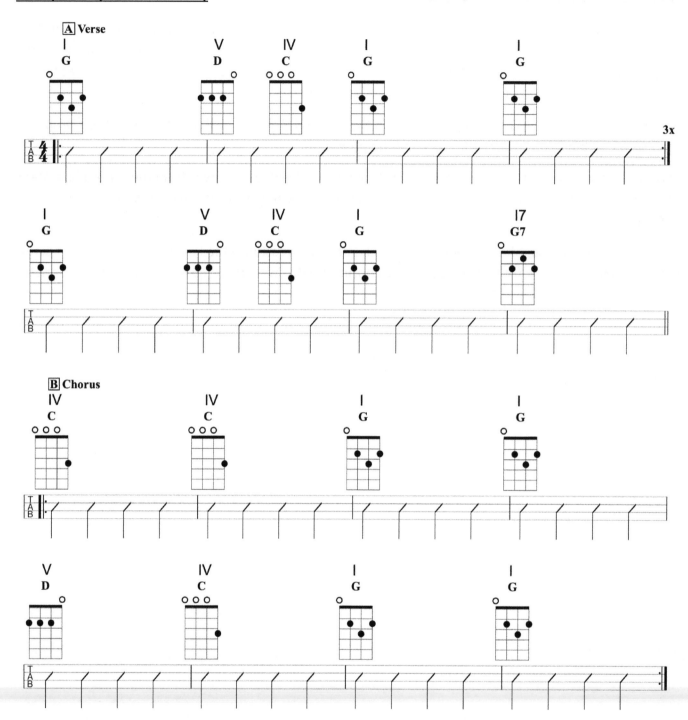

This chord progression might remind you of 'Bad Moon rising' by Creedence Clearwater Revival.

Putting it all Together

Hopefully the examples so far in this chapter have made you more aware of some of the most common song structures you might encounter. This awareness can help you see what's actually going on beneath the surface of a song. Instead of simply being a series of individual chords to be negotiated, the song can become **a series of recognisable patterns** which, with time and practice, can be absorbed into our subconsciousness and retrieved when we need them.

Let's try a little exercise which puts many of the concepts we've studied together. The piece we're going to study is in the key of D major and uses many of the musical tools and tricks seen so far in this book. Seeing them used here will be a handy reminder for you, as well as illustrating how different concepts can be made to work well together.

Before we start, here is the D major chord family. Use it for reference as we analyse the chord progression.

	I	II	III	IV	V	VI	VII
D major	D	Em	F#m	G	A	Bm	C#o

Incidentally, if this example sounds familiar, then it could be because it's very similar to the Sixties classic 'Daydream Believer'. Let's look at what's happening in the song now. We'll approach it in chunks to make it easier to see what's going on. A complete version of it will be given later for you to play if you wish. I suggest playing each part and/or listening to the audio track as you go through the analysis.

The Introduction:

Example 8.7 (Audio Track 8.7)

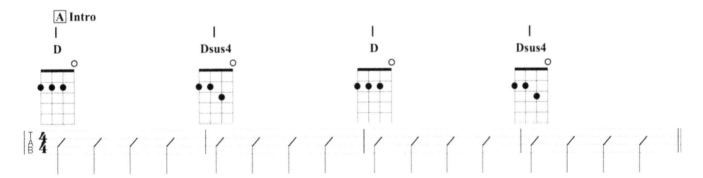

The song starts with a 4 bar intro using D and Dsus4. So, what's happening here, and what is a 'sus4' chord?

The Dsus4 is simply a D chord with a G note (2nd string 3rd fret) replacing the F# (2nd string, 2nd fret). If you check the notes in the D major scale, you'll see that G is the 4th note. In the Dsus4 chord, the 4th (G) is replacing the 3rd (F#). We could also say that the 3rd has been 'suspended' and replaced by the 4th, and as you may have guessed, 'sus' is simply shorthand for 'suspended'.

We'll talk about 'sus' chords and how they're often used later, for now just get used to the sound it creates.

The Verse:

Example 8.8 (Audio Track 8.8)

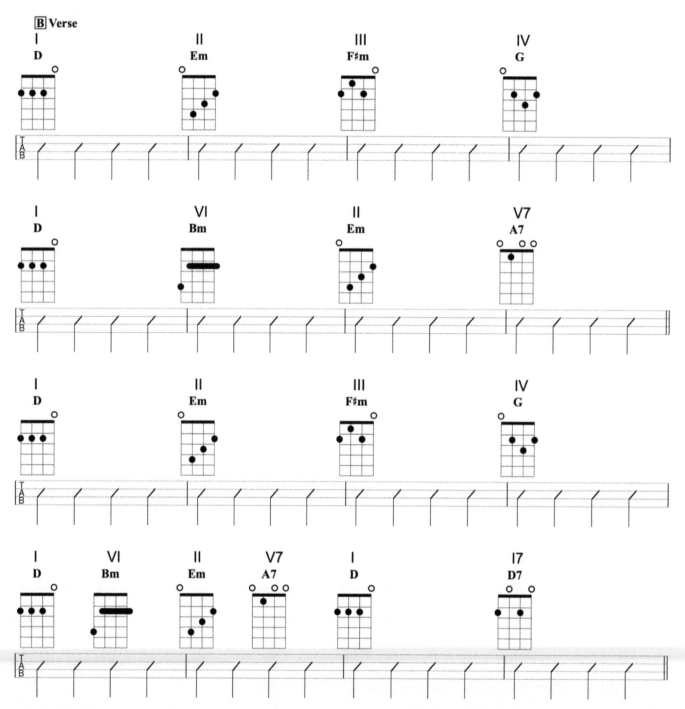

The verse employs simple chord progressions in the key of D major. The first and third lines use a I-II-III-IV progression, and in the second line we see a I-VI-II-V progression. In the fourth line of the verse we see the I-VI-II-V sequence used again, only this time it is played with 2 chords in each bar. This leads us back to D (I) before the D7 (I7) is introduced in the final bar. The D7 sets us up for a 'IV chord chorus', providing a joining chord to take us to G. This works well because D7 is the V chord of G.

The Chorus:

<u>**Example 8.9 (Audio Track 8.9)**</u>

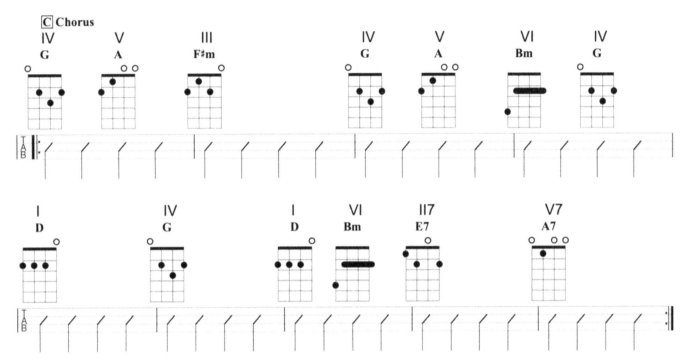

Here we have our 'IV chord chorus' starting on G (IV in the key of D). The first line of the chorus is basically going IV-V-III-IV-V-VI-IV. In the second line we're using chords I, IV, VI and V from the D major chord family. There is also a stand-in chord: E7. This is the II chord (Em) changed into a dominant7 chord and would be labelled II7. Notice the 'lift' the E7 gives the chorus, creating a moment of contrast and drama. The II7 then resolves to V (A7) which, as you might expect, leads us back to D (I).

Hopefully this all makes sense! You might want to go over this analysis again to make sure you've grasped it all, it'll help you understand many of the other songs you play.

Summary

I hope you enjoyed this longer exercise and got some benefit from doing it. It illustrates some important points:

1. The song is composed using the chord family chords, arranged into short 'building block' progressions which are combined to give the full song.
2. It uses all the chords in the D major chord family if you include the A7, which is a combination of the VII chord, C# diminished with an A root (see **Chapter 4**).
3. A stand-in II7 chord is used to give a lift to the end of the chorus.
4. It uses a 'IV chord chorus'. This is transitioned into using a I7 chord (D7).

<u>**Try this Practical Exercise**</u>

Here's the whole song laid out for you to play now. Follow the chords and the structure carefully, this is great practice for playing with other musicians. When you're ready, play it along with **audio track 8.10**.

Example 8.10 (Audio Track 8.10)

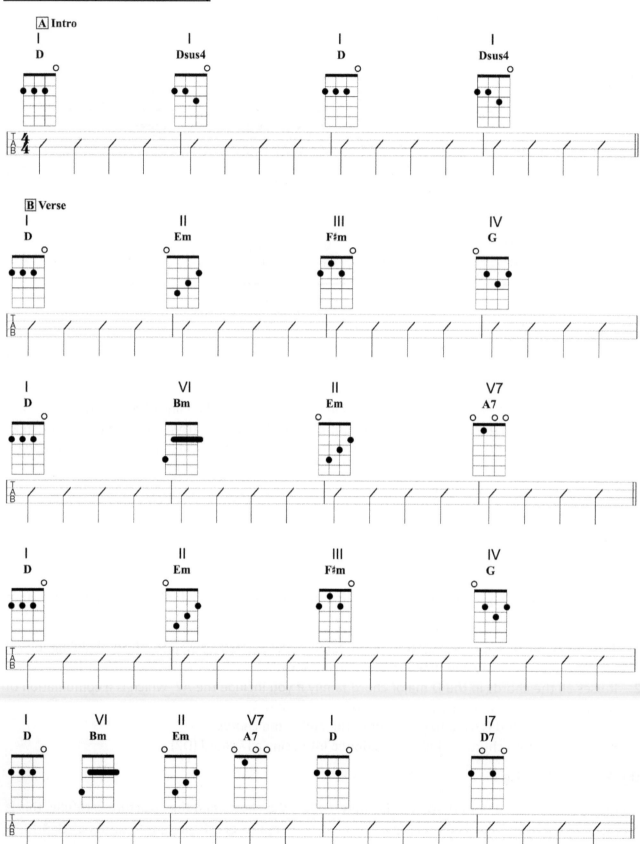

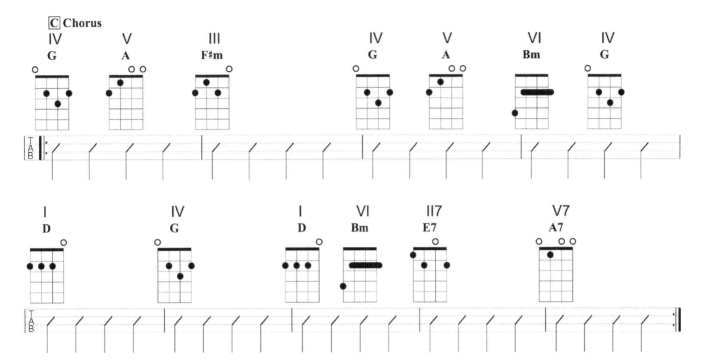

Play through twice.

That's all for this lesson on song formats…

There's quite a bit to digest in this chapter, so go over all this material again if you need to.

There's no quiz for this lesson, instead, I suggest listening to some of the songs recommended as examples. Try to recognise the **formats, chord changes and progressions** I explained in the analysis of each example.

Don't worry if the original, or version you listen to, is in a different key to the one used in the book - just concentrate on trying to follow and recognise the patterns in the songs. There are plenty of examples to play along to in this chapter.

In the next chapter we're going to look at ways of figuring out a song. We'll study how to find the key a song is in and how to use this to work out its chords. We'll also look at changing the key so that it's either easier to play or sing, or just sounds better on the uke.

So dig into this chapter, making sure you understand all the important concepts it teaches you, and when you're ready I'll see you in **Chapter 9**.

Chapter 9: Finding Keys, Transposing and Using Moveable Chord Shapes

In this chapter we're going to address some important skills you need if you want to become a more proficient uke player and musician. These will further increase your understanding of how music works, and hopefully help you to enjoy playing the uke even more, whether on your own or with others. So grab your uke, and prepare to dive into keys, transposition, and much more!

Finding the Key of a Song

Being able to find the key of a song you want to play is invaluable, making it possible to both work out, learn, and remember the song much more easily. This is the topic of the first section of this chapter. We're only going to talk about **major keys** at the moment, a more detailed look at minor keys is coming later.

So, imagine that we are listening to a song in a uke-friendly key and we want to try and work out how to play it, where would we start?

First of all we have to **find the key**. We could do this by randomly playing chords until we strike lucky, but there's a more scientific way - using our knowledge.

Using the Root of the Parent Scale to Find the Key

In **Chapter 1** we looked at the **parent scale** of a **major** key and the **chord family** we can build from it. We said that the starting point of a scale is called the **tonic** or **root note**, and the starting point of a chord is called the **root**.

If, by experimentation, we can find the **tonic** or starting point of the parent scale, then we can try to determine the **I chord** being used in the song. If we can do this, then we can use the remaining chords in the chord family to try and work out the song's chord progression. By the way, a helpful hint when looking for chord I: it's often found at the beginning and/or end of a song or each verse, so that's a good place to start looking!

Make sense?

Let's look at what to do. We'll keep this method very simple for now, to help you grasp the process. Then we'll expand on it in a minute.

1. Put on the recording of the song you want to work out the key for. Then go to the 3rd string (C string) on your uke
2. Now, play the C string as an open string and at the 1st, 2nd and 3rd frets along the neck of your uke

Some of the notes you play may sound *terrible* with the song, but you *might* hit a note which sounds like it sits quite comfortably with it. If so, then finding the key suddenly becomes much easier. You see, it's likely that this is the **tonic** or **starting note** of the **parent scale** of whichever key the song is in.

The next step is to play the I chord for the key you think you may be in. Does it sound like it also fits with the chords? Try the IV and V chords as well, do they 'sit' comfortably over some of the song? You may even find the exact chord progression by doing this exercise!

As you can see, this process has a few steps. You'll get a chance to try this out for yourself in a moment using some **recorded exercises**, but for now let's look at a few examples to avoid any confusion.

For reference, here are the notes on frets 1-3 on the C string:

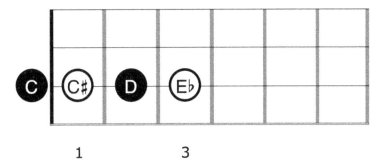

Example 1: Imagine the open **C string** is the note which sounds like it fits the best over your chosen song. There's a good chance that this is the tonic of the parent scale, **C major**. The song could therefore be in the **key of C major**. Play the I, IV and V chords (C, F and G) along with the song to see if they sound like they go with it.

Example 2: If the C string played at the **2nd fret** is the note which sounds like it fits the best then this could be the tonic of the parent scale, **D major**. The song could therefore be in the **key of D major**. Play the I, IV and V chords (D, G and A) along with the song. Do they fit?

Now, this process is not perfect, and does have some limitations, but it's a great and easy place to start with working out songs and keys. In a moment, we'll look at how to use this process to cover more situations, but first, it's time to test yourself.

Try this Practical Exercise

To practice, I've made you some exercises to try. Listen to the following **audio tracks** that come with your downloadable bonus pack (see the front of this book if you haven't got these yet).

Use the method I've shown you to work out the **key** first.

Then see if you can figure out the **chord progression** of each example (they're only using the I, IV and V chords in the chord family). You might need to refer to the 'uke-friendly' chord/key chart in **Chapter 2** to help. Good luck!

Example 9.1 (use Audio Track 9.1 for this exercise)

Example 9.2 (use Audio Track 9.2 for this exercise)

Let's See How You Did...

Example **9.1** is in the key of C major. The chord progression is shown in the following diagram:

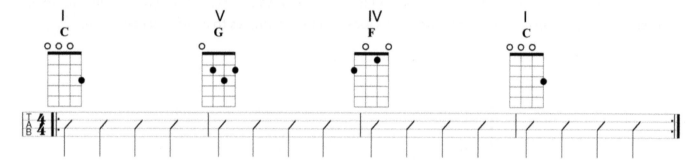

Example **9.2** is in the key of D major. The chord progression is shown in the following diagram:

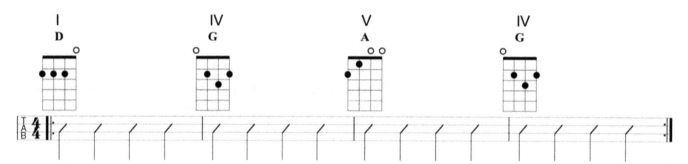

Hopefully these exercises helped you to understand how this method works, and how it's actually quite simple once you get used to it!

More Key Finding

We can use the same method to find our key using the 2nd and 1st strings. That will give us all 12 musical notes, meaning you can use this system for finding *any* of the 12 keys.

Let's look at the **E** or **2nd string** first. If the open string sounds like the tonic then our key is E. If it's one of the notes at the 1st-4th frets, then that note could be the tonic of the parent scale.

As before, you could try and find the I chord, then see if the IV and V chords fit to try and decide which key the song is in.

The next diagram shows you the notes on these frets along the 2nd string (E string).

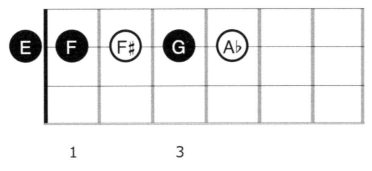

Finally, we can do the same using the **A** or **1st string**. If A sounds like the tonic, then the song is likely in the key of A major. If one of the other notes on this string sounds like the tonic then it could be in one of those keys. Whatever the case, experiment with the I, IV and V chords from the chord family to try and pinpoint some of the chord progression. Some of the notes along the A string are shown in the following diagram for reference:

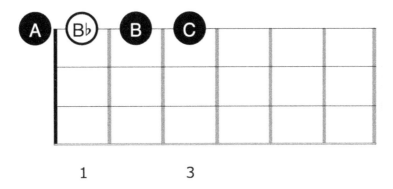

Useful Tip!

When using this method based on the **1st string** there's a really handy chord shape we can use. This is shown here:

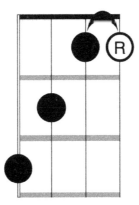

The root of this shape is on the 1st string (marked 'R' in the diagram) which means we can basically move it along the notes on the 1st string when we're trying to find the I chord. Each time we move it, we get a *different chord,* but by using the *same shape*. This is illustrated in the following diagram. If it seems a bit confusing, don't worry because we'll be looking at these kinds of moveable chord shapes very soon.

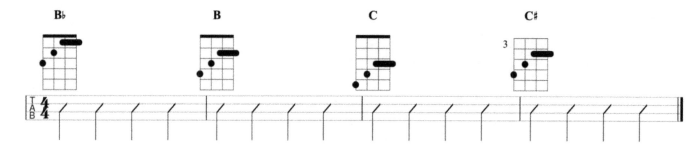

Hopefully you can see how we can try to find the key of a song using strings **1-3** and some basic chord shapes. As I said before, this is just a starting point, but a lot of the time it's enough to work out a song you want to play.

Of course, you *do* need to be able to hear and find the tonic note to use this method, and be able to hear if a chord you try fits in with the key. This is easier for some people than others, but most people can get there with a bit of practice.

Also be aware that a song may not only use chords I, IV and V as we have been doing in these examples. In this case you'll need to try some of the other chords in the chord family in order to get the whole chord progression. But getting I, IV and V is a really solid start, and as we know, those chords are likely to be in the progression somewhere.

So far, most of our key-finding study has been directed at 'uke-friendly' keys like C, D, G and A. So, what happens when we need to play in a less convenient key? There are several things we can do, but let's look at the easy one first...

Using the Capo

If we want to play along with a recording that's not in a uke-friendly key, we can use a **capo**. This is simply a mechanism that we fit to the fretboard which alters the tuning of the uke strings.

The clamped bar of the capo effectively creates a new fretboard end and raises the tuning of the strings by one semitone for each fret higher up the fretboard we move it.

For example, with the standard GCEA tuning the open strings of the uke create a C6 chord. If you fitted the capo at the first fret, everything would be raised by a semitone to give a C#6 chord. If you put the capo at the second fret, everything would be raised by two semitones to give a D6 chord.

The great thing about the capo is that we can play in a different key, but still use all the chord shapes we see in the 'uke-friendly' keys. Let's look at an example of how this works.

Here's a chord progression in the key of D:

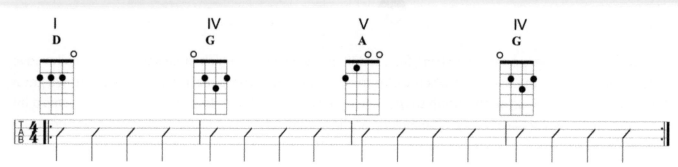

We could put the capo at the first fret and play the example exactly the same way. But, by fitting the capo at the first fret, we've actually moved all the chords up a **semitone** or **one fret**.

This means that we're actually playing E*b* (with the D shape), A*b* (with the G shape), and B*b* (with the A shape) and our key is now E*b*. We're still *thinking* in the key of D, but by raising the tuning of the uke, we now *sound* like we're playing in E*b*.

We could fit the capo at the first fret and play the following progression. We're *thinking* in the key of F here, but the capo will make it sound as if we're playing a semitone higher in the key of F#.

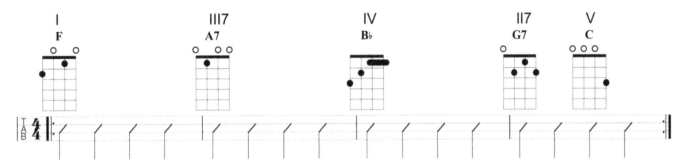

Hopefully you can see the beauty of this approach - we're using basic and familiar ukulele chord shapes which most uke players can manage to make it possible to play a progression in a less 'uke-friendly' key.

This can be used in many different ways:

- With the capo at the **1st** fret we can play in **C#** whilst *pretending* to play in **C**
- With the capo at the **1st** fret we can play in **Ab** whilst *pretending* to play in **G**
- With the capo at the **1st** fret we can play in **Eb** whilst *pretending* to play in **D**
- With the capo at the **1st** fret we can play in **Bb** whilst *pretending* to play in **A**
- With the capo at the **1st** fret we can play in **F#** whilst *pretending* to play in **F**
- With the capo at the **2nd** fret we can play in **B** whilst *pretending* to play in **A**
- With the capo at the **2nd** fret we can play in **E** whilst *pretending* to play in **D**

So, by using the capo, we can play in pretty much any key we might want to without having to get into more difficult chord shapes and chord changes. This is why so many ukulele players and guitar players love the capo!

One drawback to using the capo is that it's tempting to concentrate on playing in the 'pretend' key and we fail to think in terms of the actual chords we are using. For example, if we are trying to follow a song sheet with the chords written out in the key of E*b* but we're thinking about the chord shapes in the key of D, it can get confusing. However, it becomes better with practice.

Often you'll see the song written out in the easier key to make it more user-friendly, with the instruction to fit the capo at the required fret to 'raise' the sound of the chords to the correct key. It's much easier this way.

Try this Practical Exercise

Grab a quality ukulele capo and try out some of the simple chord progressions at the start of this book. Notice how the capo changes the key and sound of the example, even though you're still using the same chords.

Moveable Chord Shapes

The capo gives us one way to 'key shift' but there's another way which, in the long run, is more beneficial in terms of player development. This involves learning to use **moveable chord shapes**.

As we've seen, the 12 notes in the musical alphabet repeat themselves all over the ukulele neck. This means that we can combine them in various places to get chords in different zones on the fretboard. The resulting **moveable chord shapes** give us a streamlined and efficient way to play chords on the uke. You see, to play *any* of the **major** and **minor** chords in *any* of the major or minor chord families we only need **three major** and **three minor moveable chord shapes.**

This is a pretty powerful skill to master - let's take a look at how it works.

Moveable chord shapes can make a huge difference to how many chords you're able to play on the ukulele. This is because moveable shapes can be used to play *many* different chords, we just have to play them at the *correct fret* for whatever chord we need. With moveable chords it's not about memorising lots of new chord shapes, it's about getting to grips with a small number of shapes, and then learning *how* to use them.

Sometimes you might hear a player talk about **barre chords** (pronounced 'bar chords'). Generally speaking, 'barre chord' is just another name for a moveable chord played on a string instrument like a guitar or ukulele. Barre chords don't normally use any open strings, so on the uke all four strings need to be fretted. Remember the term *barre chord* for future reference, but I'll refer to them as **moveable chord shapes** for now.

Let's start by looking at three shapes we can use to play **major chords**. Pay attention to which note in each shape is the root note, this is shown as a white dot on the diagrams. This is crucially important, we'll see why shortly. Take a moment to familiarise yourself with the shapes.

Moveable Shapes for Major Chords

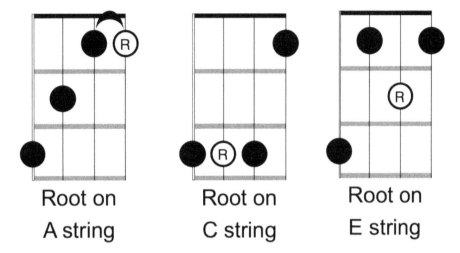

Root on
A string

Root on
C string

Root on
E string

We can adapt these shapes to get **minor chords.** See how the root notes (shown as white dots) are in the same place as before, we've simply changed the shapes slightly to get minor chords instead of major.

Moveable Shapes for Minor Chords

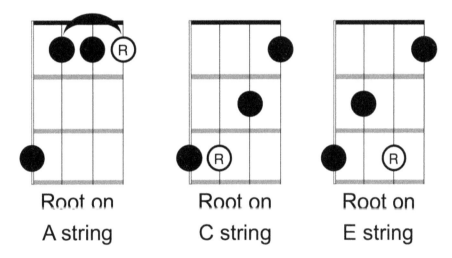

Root on
A string

Root on
C string

Root on
E string

Using Root Notes

Understanding how to use the root note is the **secret** to using moveable chord shapes. This is because we use the root note to work out *where* on the neck to play a moveable chord shape in order to get whichever chord we need. Let's look at a few examples using the movable shapes we just saw.

Refer back to the moveable **major** shape with the root on the **C string**.

If we want to use this shape to play an E♭ chord, we need to move the shape to the fret where the note on the C string becomes E♭. This is at the 3rd fret. Line the root note in the shape up with the E♭ note at the 3rd fret and we get an E♭ chord.

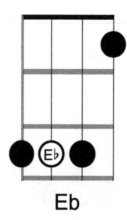

Eb

Next, look at the major shape which has its root note on the E string.

If we want to use this shape to play an F# chord, we need to move the shape to the fret where the note on the E string becomes F#. This is at the 2nd fret. Line the root note in the shape up with the F# note at the 2nd fret and we get an F# chord.

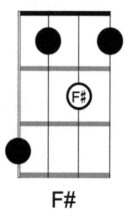

F#

Next, look at the major shape which has its root note on the A string.

If we want to use this shape to play a C# chord, we need to move the shape to the fret where the note on the A string becomes C#. This is at the 4th fret. Line the root note in the shape up with this fret and we get a C# chord.

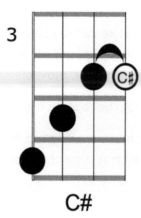

C#

Here are the notes along the G, C and E strings up to the 5th fret. Using these we can work out where to play any of our moveable major chord shapes in order to get any major chord. These are shown in the example following the fretboard diagram.

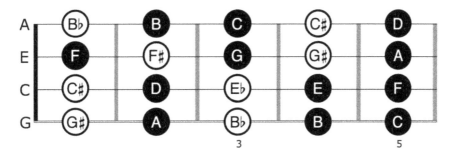

Moveable minor chords work in the exact same way, simply use the minor shapes instead. We can then use them to derive any minor chord we might need.

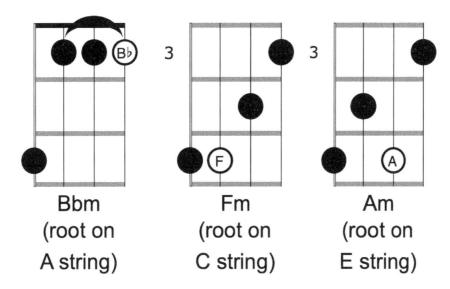

In *theory*, all these moveable chord shapes can be played anywhere on the fretboard to get any major and minor chord, but as you get higher up the fretboard they become increasingly difficult to play. I've chosen to show you what I think is the most practical application for each shape in this lesson, focusing on the area around the 1st to 5th frets.

Moveable Chords and Key Families

As you've probably noticed, moveable chord shapes allow us to play chords which we simply can't play with simple open chord shapes. This means we can now play in some of the less 'uke-friendly' keys.

The following examples show you how to play chords I, II, III, IV, V and VI in a few different keys (we're going to ignore the VII chord for now). Play each one, studying how the moveable chord shapes are being used.

Key of **B♭ major** - the I chord is being played using the moveable major shape with the root on the A string.

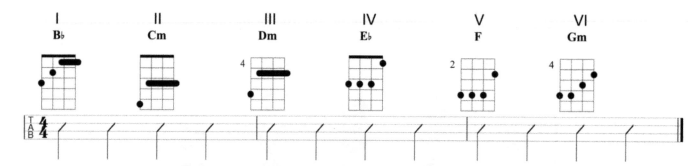

Key of **Eb major** - the I chord is being played using the moveable major shape with the root on the E string.

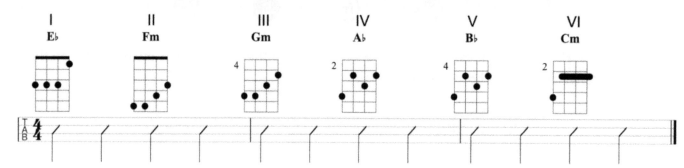

Let's try some examples of common chord progressions using these patterns. Practice each one, listening to the sound of it as you play it. Hopefully you're starting to recognise some of these common chord progressions a bit by now. When you're ready, try playing each one along with the audio tracks.

This first example is a I-VI-IV-V progression in the key of B major:

Example 9.3 (Audio Track 9.3)

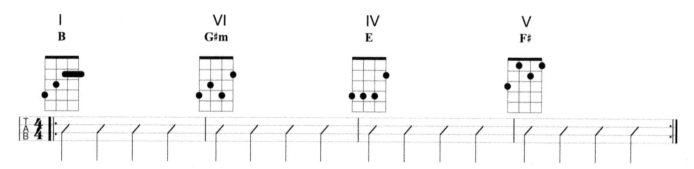

The following example uses moveable shapes to play a I-VI-II-V progression in the key of A*b* major:

Example 9.4 (Audio Track 9.4)

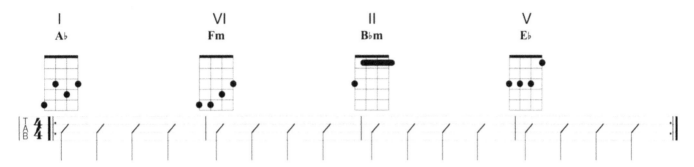

Now we'll play a I-VI-IV-V progression in the key of Eb major:

Example 9.5 (Audio Track 9.5)

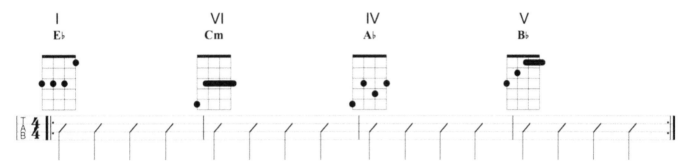

As you play these examples, pay attention to the different combinations of moveable shapes we are using. Getting to grips with these will really help you master using moveable chord shapes in your playing.

Movable Dominant 7th Shapes

Let's look at three moveable shapes you can use for playing dominant7 chords. These work in exactly the same way as the major and minor shapes do. I suggest mentally relating them to the moveable major shapes to make them easier to remember. Of course, make sure to learn which note is the root note in all these shapes.

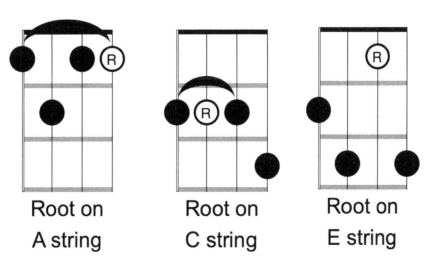

We can also use the open G7 shape. The root note for this shape is on the 4th or G string.

Sometimes, to make the shape easier, you may want to miss the 4th string off (even though it's the string with the root note).

The chord will still work well, even without the root being played! When omitting this string, consider muting it slightly with your fret hand thumb to keep it quiet.

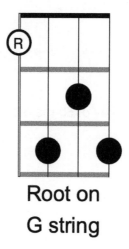

Root on
G string

Let's look at combining these dominant7 shapes to play a common chord progression.

Listen carefully to the sound they give you and play along with the audio track when you're ready to.

Example 9.6 (Audio Track 9.6)

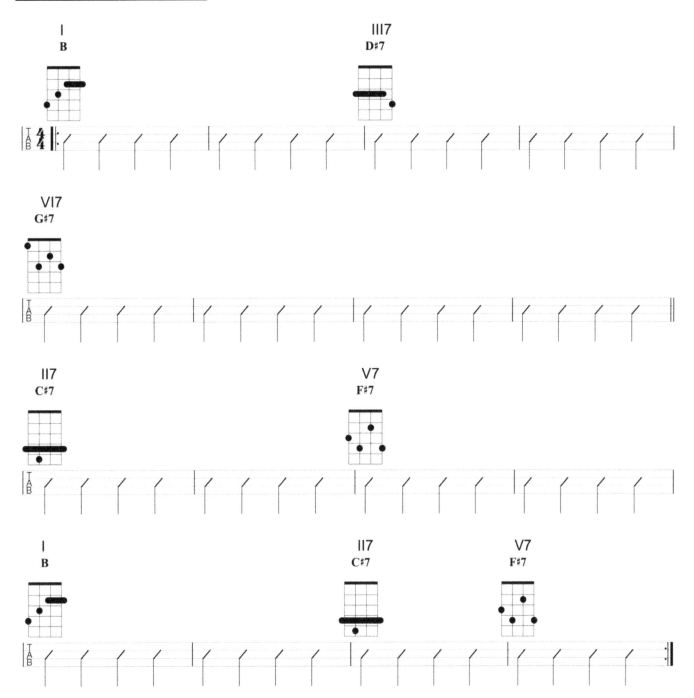

Where do Moveable Chords Come From?

From experience helping other players, I've found that many of them fail to make the connection between moveable shapes and the 'everyday' open chords they use all the time. So, now that you're familiar with moveable chord shapes, let's look at where they come from.

Moveable chord shapes are simply what we get when we slide *every string* in one of our 'everyday' chord shapes higher up the fretboard. Notice I said *every* string! This includes any **open** strings in the original chord shape. These are part of the makeup of the chord, and also need to be moved along with the notes we are pressing down with our fretting hand.

Look at the moveable shape with the root note on the C string. Here it's used to play an Eb chord. Look closely and you'll see it's simply our open D chord moved up 1 fret:

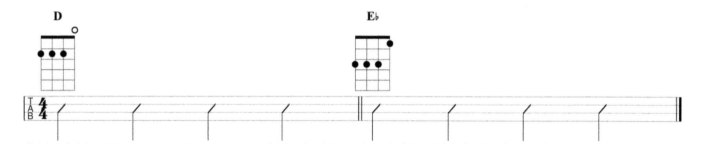

Note that when moved down a semitone, the open 1st string replaces the fretted note at the 1st fret, giving the open D shape chord.

This moveable shape is being used to play a Bb chord. Look carefully and you can see it's simply the open A chord shape with each string moved up 1 fret:

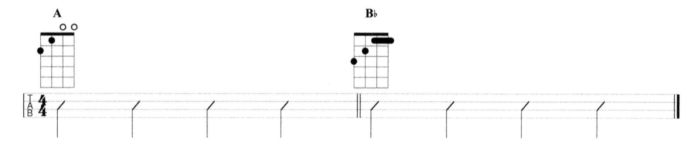

Hopefully you get the idea. Here are some of the other moveable shapes shown side by side with the open chords they are derived from. Study these diagrams carefully and you'll see the connection between each pair of shapes.

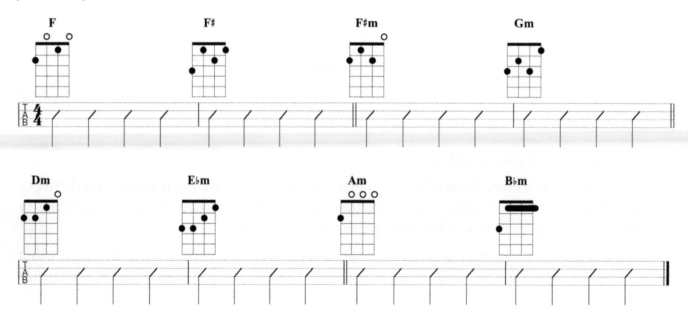

Before we leave the topic of moveable chords, here's a bonus shape! It comes from our open C chord shape and the root is on the C string. Here it's being used to play a C# chord:

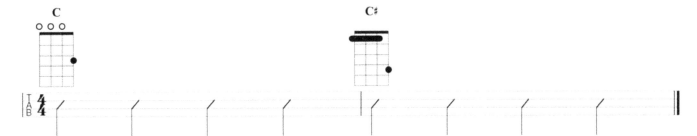

Ok, that just about covers our major, minor and dominant7 movable chord shapes. There are some other useful chords we can play with moveable shapes, and we'll take a look at some of these later. For now, the most important thing to do is study these shapes and get to grips with how they work. Make sure you *thoroughly* understand how the root notes in the shapes tell us where to play them for any chord - this concept really is essential!

Understanding and being able to fluently use moveable chords is a *big* breakthrough for any uke player who wants to take their playing to the next level. So consider pausing a while to thoroughly digest all this material before you move on to the next part of the chapter.

Try this Practical Exercise

The following diagram shows you the circle of fifths. This is an amazing practice tool! Starting on C at the top, play **clockwise** around the circle.

Using one of our moveable chord shapes, play a **major** chord starting on each note you come to as you travel around the circle. In other words, you'll play **C**, then **G**, then **D**, then **A** - and so on, as you work your way around the circle.

Then, repeat the exercise playing **minor** chords.

If you spend a little time with this exercise, I guarantee you, one day soon you'll be at uke practice and will notice you're able to play nearly all the chords you encounter in the songs you play. This is the power of these moveable shapes. Good luck!

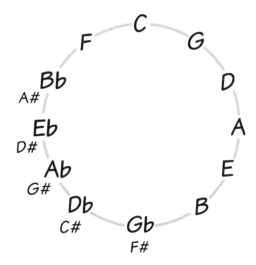

Transposing Chord Sequences

To finish this chapter, let's study how to change the chord progressions of a song from one key to another. If you've understood what we've covered until now this shouldn't be too difficult.

So far in this book we've used Roman numerals to describe each of the chords in a chord family built from the notes in the parent scale. These are what we are going to use when we want to move, or **transpose**, a chord progression into a new key.

Probably the most common reason for wanting to do this is to accommodate a vocalist and their natural range, but as a uke player, it could also be to make the chords easier to play in a group of mixed abilities.

Here's an example chord sequence in the key of B♭ major. Pay special attention to the Roman numeral analysis, we'll use this to transpose it into a new key in a moment.

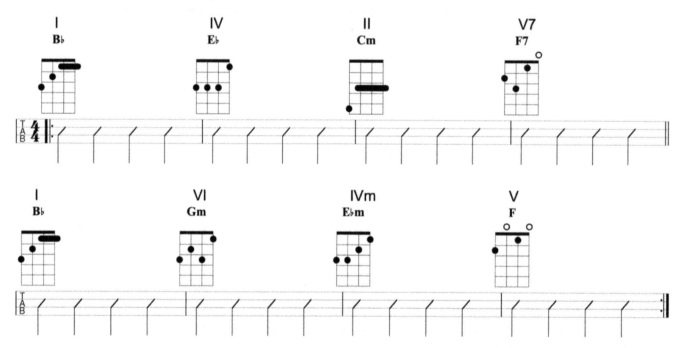

Let's transpose the chord progression into the key of D major. All we have to do is find the Roman numeral notations for the chords in the original key and substitute the corresponding chords from the new key.

This is shown in the following diagram. The D major chord family is shown for reference too, study it with the new progression to help you make sense of this concept.

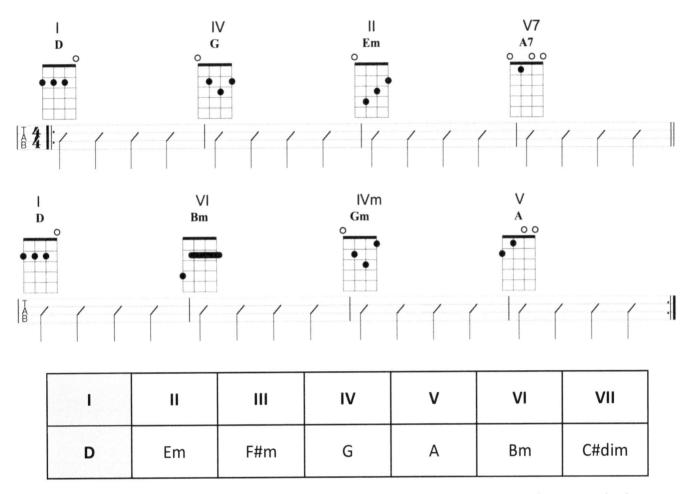

I	II	III	IV	V	VI	VII
D	Em	F#m	G	A	Bm	C#dim

Here's another example using some stand-in chords. Notice how the process works in exactly the same way as when we're only using chords in the chord family. Simply use the Roman numerals to work out the transposed stand-in chords. Key of C:

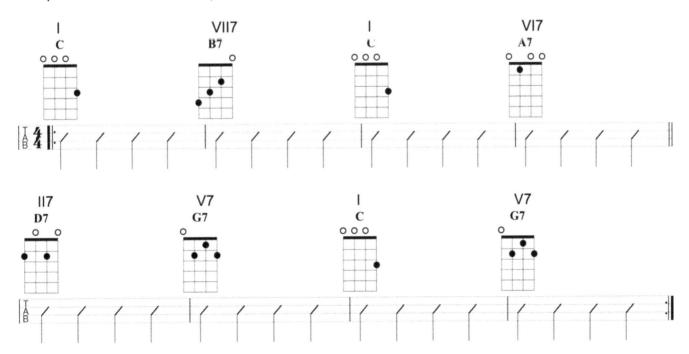

Transposed into the key of F:

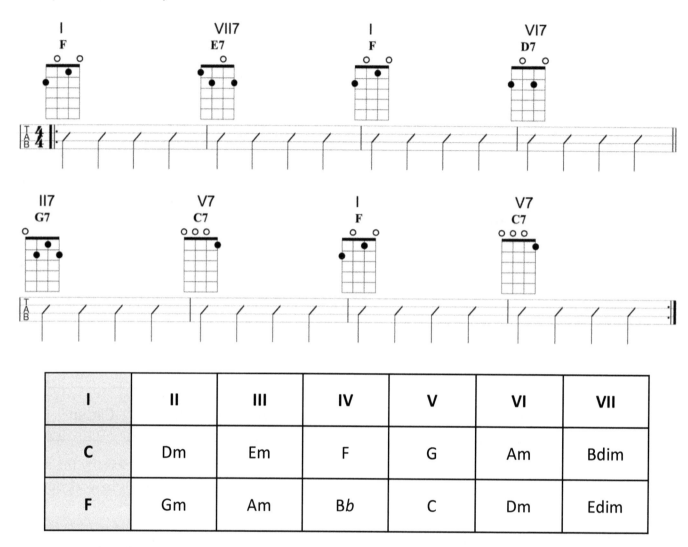

I	II	III	IV	V	VI	VII
C	Dm	Em	F	G	Am	Bdim
F	Gm	Am	B*b*	C	Dm	Edim

You can see that the process is actually quite simple:

1. Simply find the position of each chord (identified by its Roman numeral) in the original key
2. Substitute the corresponding chords from the new key. It doesn't matter what the type of chord is - minor, major, dominant 7, augmented 5th, sus4 or anything else, the approach remains the same

That's all for this lesson…

We've covered a lot of important concepts in this chapter, so well done if you feel like you've got to grips with most of this information.

I'm betting you're going to need to go over some of this material again, so revisit any sections you need to. Don't be in a rush, most players take *years* to discover what I've shown you in this chapter! I'd definitely recommend devoting some practice time to moveable chords - they're so incredibly useful.

Test yourself with the quiz when you're ready, have fun, and I'll see you in the next chapter.

Quick Quiz

1. When we talk about scales, what do we mean by the **tonic**?

2. The tonic is the root of which number chord in a chord family? (Answer using a Roman numeral)

3. Look at these chord shapes. Identify which note is the root note in each shape.

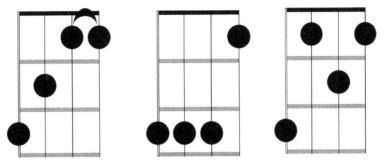

4. Using your knowledge of moveable chord shapes and root notes, identify the following chords.

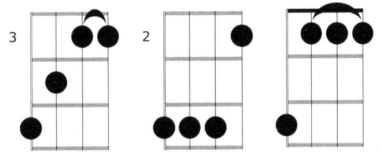

5. Your uke is in standard tuning (G-C-E-A). You put a capo at the 1st fret. What notes do your open strings become?

6. Using the major key chord family chart in **Chapter 2**, transpose this progression from the key of D major into the key of A major (use Roman numeral identification to help).

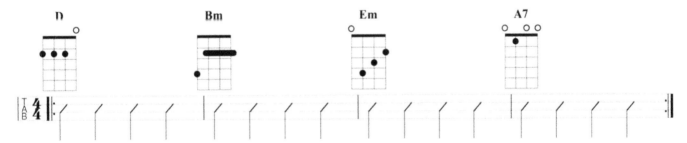

7. The following chord progression is in the key of F major. Transpose it into the key of A major.

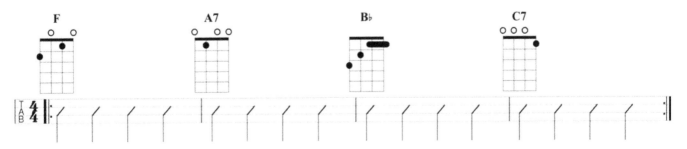

Check Your Answers

1. The **tonic** is the starting point of a scale, or first note in a scale. We could also call it a root note.

2. The tonic is the root of the **I chord** in the chord family.

3. The root notes for the chord shapes are shown on the following diagrams.

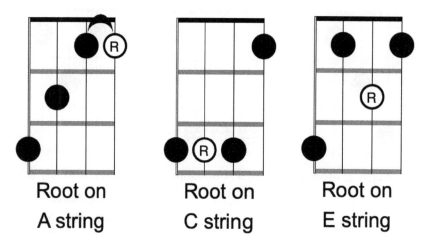

Root on   Root on   Root on
A string   C string   E string

4. The chords you get when you play the given moveable chord shapes are as follows:

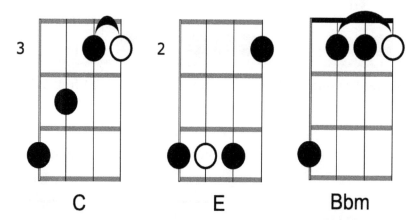

C   E   Bbm

5. If you placed the capo at the 1st fret on your uke, the open string notes would be a semitone higher than standard tuning. They would go from G-C-E-A to **G#-C#-F-A#**.

6. The chord progression in C is a I-VI-II-V7 progression. In the key of A it would be this:

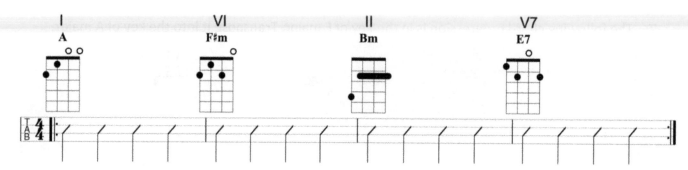

7. *The chord progression in F major is a I-III7-IV-V progression. Transposed into the key of A it would become:*

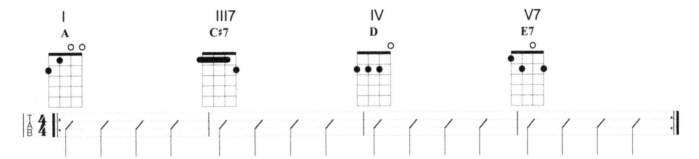

Chapter 10: Minor Keys

We've talked about major keys a lot in this book, and you hopefully feel like you have a good understanding of what major keys are and what we can do with them. The trouble is, lots of songs are in minor keys, *not* major keys!

In this chapter we'll take a look at the topic of minor keys. The good news is this: if you've thoroughly worked through all the previous lessons in this book, then getting to grips with minor keys is going to be pretty easy.

So grab your uke, as we look at minor key chord families, minor key chord progressions, and more.

What is a Minor Key?

We've seen how a major key is basically a set of chords - we've been calling it a chord family. This comes from a particular major scale, which we called the parent scale.

Minor keys are based on exactly the same idea, the difference is that the parent scale is *not* the major scale, instead we use the **Natural Minor** scale. The natural minor scale sounds different to the major scale, and this is what gives us the distinctive darker, more melancholy sound of minor keys.

Just to be clear, we are **not** using any new notes to make a minor key, natural minor scales and minor chord families still *only* use the notes in the musical alphabet. The notes are arranged in a different way though, and that's what creates the difference between the sound of major and minor scales and chord families.

So, how do we figure out what chords to use in a minor key? Well, we need to go back to the relative minor key concept we discussed earlier in the book. This makes learning about minor keys easy.

Relative Keys and Chord Families

Back in **Chapter 6** we saw how each major key has a very closely-related minor key. This is called the **relative minor key**. We also saw how the chord families for any major key and its relative minor key are **the same**. This makes it *much* easier to become familiar with minor key chord families. Let's look at how this works in more detail.

The relative minor chord/key is always chord VI in a major chord family.

Study the following table showing the C major chord family:

I	II	III	IV	V	VI	VII
C	Dm	Em	F	G	Am	Bdim

See how chord VI is A minor? This tells us that A minor is the relative minor key of C major.

Parent Scales

We'll return to chord families in a moment, but first let's take a quick look at the parent scales for a major key and it's relative minor key. The first thing to know is that both parent scales contain exactly the same notes, they're just in a different order. We can see this by looking at the C major scale and its relative minor scale, A natural minor:

C major scale: **C D E F G A B C**

A natural minor: **A B C D E F G A**

If we take these notes and think of **C** as the **tonic** or root, we get the **C major scale**.

If we take the same notes but make **A** into the **tonic**, we get the **A natural minor scale**.

This simple shifting around of the notes creates two scales with a remarkably different sound, even though the notes they contain are identical - amazing!

So how come exactly the same notes produce two different sounding scales? It's all to do with which note we *emphasise*. If we arrange these notes around C and think of it as the tonic, we place the emphasis on C. This causes us to *hear* the notes in terms of how they *sound* in relation to C.

Take the same notes but place the emphasis on A by making A the tonic, and we *hear* the notes in terms of how they relate to A.

Chord Families and the Relative Minor

We've already said that the chord families for a major key and its relative minor key are the same. So, you're probably wondering: why don't these two chord families sound exactly the same as each other?

It all comes down to which chord we emphasise and arrange the other chords around when we build them into progressions. The following table shows you the chords in the A minor chord family. Compare it to the C major chord family shown a moment ago - what do you notice?

I	II	III	IV	V	VI	VII
Am	Bdim	C	Dm	Em	F	G

Hopefully you're able to spot two things:

1. The chords are the same
2. The Am chord is now acting as the I chord in the family. The emphasis is therefore placed on the A minor chord, the C major chord is simply one of the other chords in the family

This relationship between major and relative minor keys applies for **all keys**, so no matter which major and relative minor keys you choose, the chords in their chord families will both be the **same**.

This is a handy shortcut, it means we can take our 'uke-friendly' keys and pair them with their relative minors to play in minor keys, all without needing to learn any new chords or chord families.

Here are our pairs of related keys:

Major Key	Relative Minor key
C major	A minor
G major	E minor
F major	D minor
D major	B minor
A major	F# minor

We can now take the major key chord family for each of these, and by starting it on chord VI, get the chord family for the related minor key. The resulting minor key chord families are shown in the following table. Cross check them with the major key families shown in the table in **Chapter 2** to see the connection.

I	II	III	IV	V	VI	VII
Am	Bdim	C	Dm	Em	F	G
Em	F#dim	G	Am	Bm	C	D
Dm	Edim	F	Gm	Am	Bb	C
Bm	C#dim	D	Em	F#m	G	A
F#m	G#dim	A	Bm	C#m	D	E

Minor key chord families consist of minor *and* major chords, so playing in a minor key does **not** mean *all* the chords we use are going to be minor. There are some exceptions, but most songs use a mixture of minor and major chords even if they're in a minor key.

Important note: the topic of minor keys can get quite complex and confusing because there are actually *several* possible chord families for each minor key! Some people also use different slightly Roman numeral methods to describe chord progressions in minor keys. We're going to simplify the topic a little to avoid the confusing bits, most of which you don't need to know anyway. This chapter will give you more than enough information to understand most minor key songs you'll probably ever play on your ukulele.

Using V7 Chords in Minor Keys

In a moment we're going to hear and play some minor key chord progressions, but first I want to briefly talk about something you'll often encounter when playing in minor keys.

Look at the V chord in the chord family chart we just studied. Notice how it's a minor chord (Vm). It's very common to see this chord *changed* into a **dominant7** or **V7** chord.

The reason is that, just like in major keys, the V7 has a magnetic 'pull' which can be used to take us back to the minor I chord (Im). Sometimes the V chord is simply changed into a major chord instead of a dominant7, creating a similar level of 'pull' back to the Im.

This gives us **three** variations of the V-I chord movement (or *perfect cadence*) when playing in minor keys:

Vm-Im

Vmaj-Im

V7-Im

Look out for all these in the songs you play, you'll see them *all* being used. Let's hear the sounds they give us now. Remember to use the 'PLAY, LISTEN, HEAR' approach, at least some of the time, as you work through these examples. This will train your ears to recognise and remember some common minor key sounds.

This progression in the key of E minor is using the minor V chord (Vm).

Example 10.1 (Audio Track 10.1)

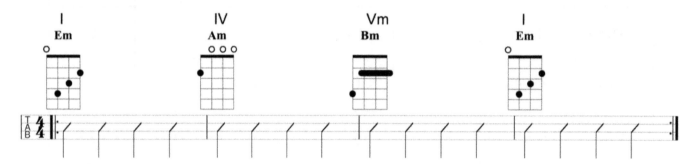

Let's contrast this with the sound of the Vmaj and V7 chords heard in this next example.

Example 10.2 (Audio Track 10.2)

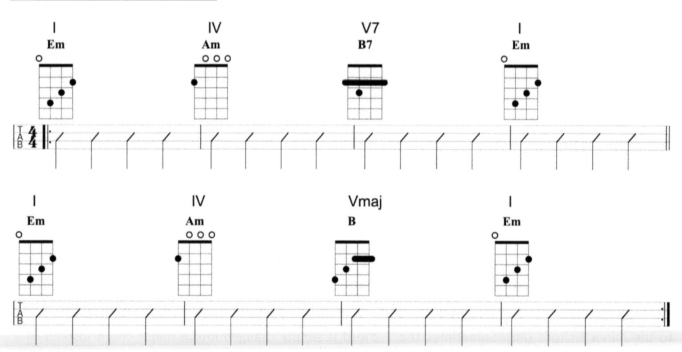

You can probably hear how the Vmaj and V7 chords create a much stronger 'pull' towards the minor I chord. This is why songwriters will often (but not always!) use them instead of the Vm option.

You can think of the Vmaj and V7 chords as stand-in chords for the time being (although there are some more accurate reasons why they work). Oh, and whilst on the subject of stand-in chords, you may sometimes see the minor IV chord (IVm) changed to **IV maj** or **IV7**. Just be aware of this in case you encounter it from time to time.

Try this Practical Exercise

Choose one of the minor key families in the table you were given a moment ago.

Now practice playing the V-I chord movement in the key, using the Vm chord which occurs naturally in the chord family.

Now replace the Vm chord with a Vmaj chord and a V7 chord, listening carefully to the difference in sound. Do you prefer one of the V chord options over the others?

Minor Key Progressions and Variations

Before we look at some more minor key chord progressions, I know that some readers out there will be thinking:

If the chords we use are the same for a major key and its related minor key, then surely chord progressions in both these keys sound the same?

Nope! We touched on this briefly a moment ago, but let's clarify something important. It's all to do with that word *emphasis* again. The chords in the C major and A minor chord families *are the same* chords because the two keys are related, but we would *use* them in different ways depending on which key we were in.

To put it simply, in C major we would make the C chord sound like the 'main chord' in the progression. In the key of A minor, we'd frame the Am chord so that *it* sounded like the main chord. So depending on which chord we emphasise, our chord progression might sound like it's in the key of C major, or A minor.

Play the following examples and listen carefully to the audio tracks to clearly hear the difference between the major and minor key. The chords in these progressions are almost identical, but the emphasis is placed on a different chord to create a different musical effect.

Example 10.3 (Audio Track 10.3)

Key of C major (emphasis on C chord)

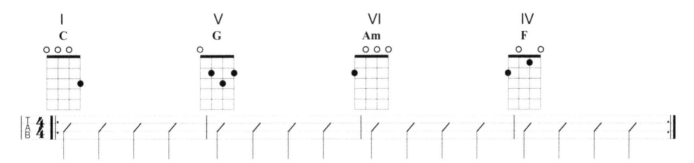

Example 10.4 (Audio Track 10.4)

Key of A minor (emphasis on Am chord)

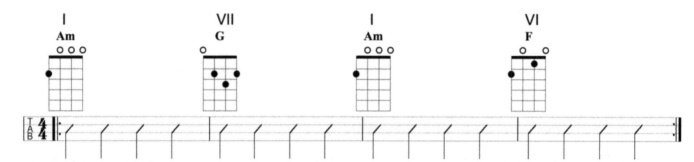

Hopefully all this makes perfect sense. Next, we'll look at some minor key progressions like the ones we see in many popular ukulele songs. Refer to the minor key chord family chart from a moment ago as you work through these examples, it'll help you to understand what's happening in the music.

Minor Progression with V7 Chord

Singer-songwriter Leonard Cohen often favours the darker, sadder sound of a minor key. This next example might remind you of his song 'Dance Me To The End of Love'. This example is in the key of E minor and uses mainly the Im and IVm chords, but notice the use of the V7 chord too. I think the V7 chord lends a Spanish or 'gypsy' mood to the chord progression.

Listen to the audio and try playing along when you're ready. I'm using a 'down-down, up-down-down, up' strumming rhythm on the audio track, listen to it to hear this.

Example 10.5 (Audio Track 10.5)

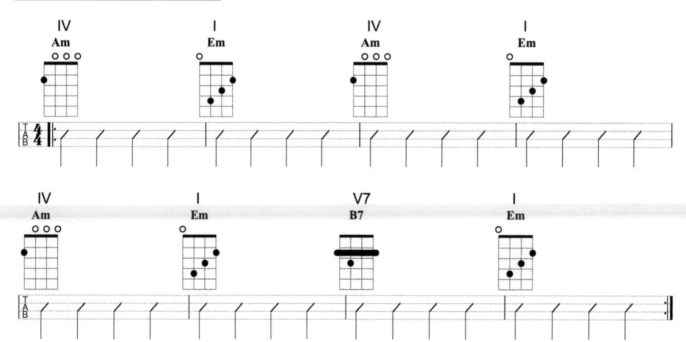

The *'Andalusian Cadence'*

There's a Spanish sounding chord progression used in flamenco music that's very recognisable and has been adapted over the years to form the basis of many classic songs. It's written out in the following example in the key of D minor. Notice how the V7 chord at the end is used to return to the I chord when we repeat the sequence. Play this and listen carefully to the descending notes within the chords, they're easy to hear and are an important part of learning to recognise this progression.

Example 10.6 (Audio Track 10.6)

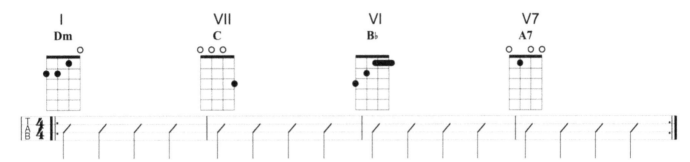

Make sure to use the 'PLAY, LISTEN, HEAR' practice exercise for this progression, it's used a lot and doing this will help you to recognise it. This chord progression is sometimes referred to as the 'Andalusian Cadence' and can be described as a **I–VII–VI–V7** in a minor key.

This common chord sequence has been used in many songs from all different eras: Frankie Laine's 'Jezebel' in the 1950's, Del Shannon's 'Runaway' in the 1960's, Dire Straits' 'Sultans of Swing' in the 1980's, and from the late 1990's, Christine Aguilera's 'Genie in a Bottle'. Listen to recordings of some of these songs to hear what I mean.

The *'Andalusian Cadence'* with Variations

This next example is similar to the Andalusian Cadence, but it's had a few extra twists added. It reminds me of 'Knock, Knock' by Jack Savoretti, but you'll hear it used in hundreds of other songs as well.

It's shown in the key of A minor. Listen carefully and study the Roman numeral analysis to help it make sense. Play along with the audio track to practice.

Example 10.7 (Audio Track 10.7)

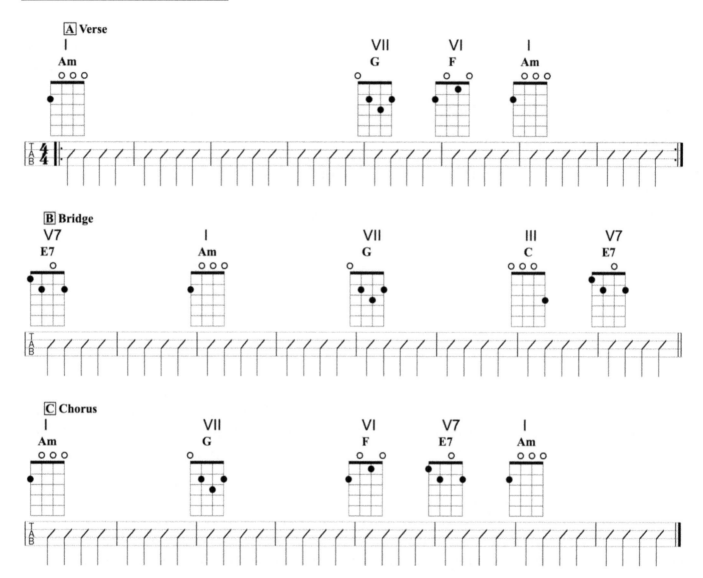

There's no doubt about it, this progression conveys the dark and 'moody' feel of a minor key. But notice how it only uses *one* minor chord: Am. This chord has been 'framed' in a way that gives us the distinctive minor key sound, even though all the other chords in the progression are major or dominant7. Once again, it's all to do with that word - **emphasis**!

Try this Practical Exercise

Choose one of the minor key chord families shown in the table earlier in this chapter.

Now, work out which chords would be used to play the Andalusian Cadence in this key. Play the progression on your ukulele. You can also experiment with some different tempos and rhythms as you do this exercise. Don't overthink it, just get creative and try out different possibilities!

Repeat this Andalusian Cadence exercise for some other minor keys.

A Classic Minor Key Progression

One of the iconic minor key songs in the uke repertoire is the old blues/folk song '*House of the Rising Sun*'. If ever there was a song about 'hard times', then this has to be it, and a minor key suits the mood perfectly.

The chord progression is shown next in the key of D minor. Once again, it uses very few minor chords, despite the dramatic, sombre mood it conveys. The minor I chord is 'framed' to create the minor key effect and a V7 chord is used to create even more drama. Notice too how the sequence also uses a IVmaj chord (G) as a stand-in for the usual IVm chord in the key of D minor (which would be Gm).

Listen to the audio track to hear the sound of this progression and play it on your ukulele. When you're ready, put on the audio track and practice playing along. This is great practice for when you play with other people.

One more thing, this progression is in **3/4** ('three four') time. This means there are **3 beats in each bar** instead of the usual four beats per bar. Listen to the audio to hear this, and get an idea of how you might strum it. Have fun!

Example 10.8 (Audio Track 10.8)

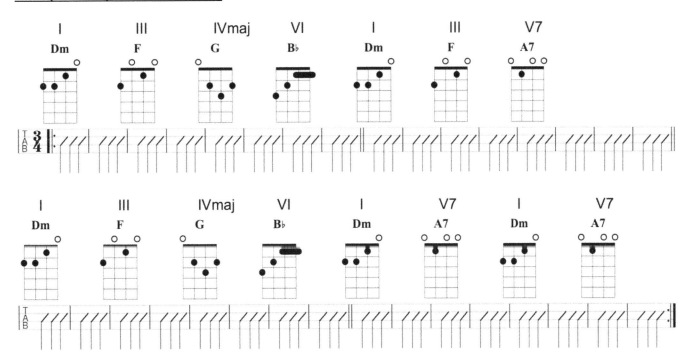

Minor Keys: Quick Recap

Let's quickly review some of the key points we've examined so far in this chapter on minor keys:

1. Minor chord families are built from the **natural minor scale** and contain both minor and major chords
2. The chords in a minor key chord family are the **same** as in the **related major key** (the relative minor - relative major connection)
3. We can use **stand-in** major or dominant 7 chords to replace the minor IV or minor V chords

4. By 'framing' the Im chord in a strong way, we can create the sound of a minor key, even if many of the chords in a progression are actually major

5. Most minor key songs will use a mixture of minor and major chords. Often these will include a stand-in V7 chord

If you're not sure about some of these points, consider reading about them again until you feel a bit more confident. Otherwise, we'll carry on.

The Vm Chord

We haven't seen a minor V chord used in a song yet, but these do occur, so we'll look at an example now. This next chord progression is in the key of Em and is using Bm as its V chord. We'll label this **Vm** just to highlight the fact that it's minor. Notice the more sombre, slightly darker feel this creates compared to when we use a Vmaj or V7 chord.

Example 10.9 (Audio Track 10.9)

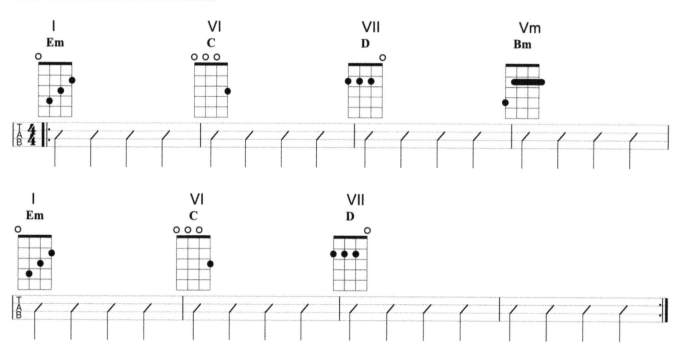

This progression is a bit like the chords to 'Let Her Go' by Passenger, a popular song in the modern uke repertoire.

Occasionally, the minor V chord is 'borrowed' from a minor key and used in a major key. This is pretty rare, but it's worth mentioning whilst we're on this topic. Our example is in the key of A major.

Instead of the Vmaj or V7 chord you might expect (E or E7), we've got a **Vm** chord. This adds a surprising twist to an otherwise predictable chord progression. Play the example and listen to the audio track to hear the effect.

Also play it with the major V or V7 chord instead so you can hear the difference.

Example 10.10 (Audio Track 10.10)

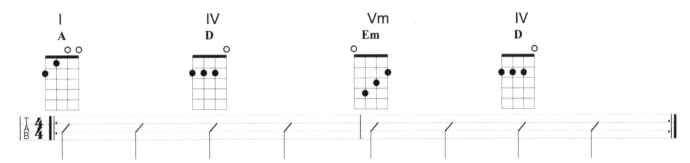

Notice the difference this makes? One song that uses a Vm chord is 'Louie, Louie' by The Kingsmen. Listen to this to hear a real-life example of the Vm chord being used.

As a reminder, use the 'PLAY, HEAR, LISTEN' approach with all these examples. Doing this will help you learn to recognise the different V chord options and sounds. It might not happen overnight, but be patient and you'll start to see your ear improve, I promise!

That's all for this lesson...

Our aim in this chapter is really to learn to recognise and understand the common minor key progressions encountered in the uke repertoire. What we've covered should enable you to do this, so from a purely practical point of view, there's probably not a lot more to say on the subject of minor keys.

We've slightly simplified some of the concepts here, but bear in mind that there are sound music theory reasons why all the things we've looked at work - none of this is a random process. Instead of diving deep into all sorts of theory concepts (most of which you'll probably never need), I've tried to encourage you to listen and learn to identify common traits we see in minor keys. This will be of immense value to you when you play with other musicians.

Test yourself with the quiz that follows, and when you're ready I'll see you in the next chapter where we're going to be looking at some interesting ways to make our regular uke chords a bit more attention-grabbing. See you then!

Quick Quiz

1. The chord family for a minor key is built from which scale?

2. Any major key shares the same notes and chord family with which other key?

3. Which keys use the same notes and chord families as G major and D major?

4. Which keys use the same notes and chord families as A minor and F# minor?

5. What are the 3 common chord qualities used for playing the V chord in minor keys?

6. Which other minor chord in a minor key chord family is sometimes replaced with a stand-in chord?

Check Your Answers

1. The chord family for a minor key is built from the **natural minor scale**.

2. Any major key shares the same notes and chord family with its **relative minor key**. This is the minor key built from chord **VI** in the major key chord family.

3. The keys which use the same notes and chord families as G major and D major are **E minor** (relative minor of G) and **B minor** (relative minor of D).

4. The keys which use the same notes and chord families as A minor and F# minor are **C major** (relative major of Am) and **A major** (relative major of F#m).

5. The 3 common chord qualities used for playing the V chord in minor keys are **major (Vmaj)**, **dominant7 (V7)** and **minor (Vm)**.

6. The **IVm** chord in a minor chord family is often replaced by a **major** stand-in chord. This would be described with the label **IVmaj** (sometimes just written as **IV**).

Chapter 11: 'Messing about' with Chords

If you've used a song sheet or song book before, then you've probably come across chords which you didn't know how to play. Some of them probably had names like Dm7, C6, Fmaj7 or Esus4. Perhaps you know a few shapes for playing these kinds of chords, but what are these more 'advanced' chords doing? What do they sound like, and how can we learn to recognise them?

Normally chords like these are simply a **decorated** version of something simpler, like a major or minor chord. Other times, they're in the song to perform a specific musical job or function.

In this chapter we're going to examine some of these different types of chords so that when you see them in a song they don't catch you out. You'll also be able to 'mess about' with the chords of a song and make it sound a little different if you want to! You really *don't* need to be an expert on complex chords to enjoy doing this on the uke, but a little practical knowledge will be very helpful.

So grab your uke, and we'll get started.

Triads

I covered triads in detail in my *Music Theory for Ukulele* book, but let's take a quick look at them now.

A **triad** is simply a chord containing 3 notes. Most of the chords we play on the uke, simple major and minor chords like C, G, Em, or Dm, are triads. Let's have a quick look at how basic major and minor triads are built.

We can think of **major** triads as coming from the major scale. We simply group together the **root** (1st note), **3rd** and **5th** notes in the scale and we get a **major triad**

In the C major scale this is the notes C, E and G, giving us a C major triad. You can see this in the table and C major chord shape shown.

Root	2nd	3rd	4th	5th	6th	7th
C	D	E	F	G	A	B

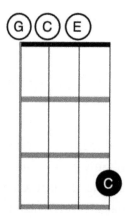

If we group together the **root**, **3rd** and **5th** notes from the natural minor scale we get a **minor triad**. Applying this to the G natural minor scale gives us a G minor triad. The following table and Gm chord shape illustrates this:

G	A	B*b*	C	D	E*b*	F

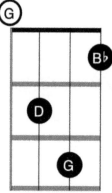

The ukulele has 4 strings, but triads only contain 3 notes. For this reason, when we play triads on the uke one of the notes is normally repeated. Look at the notes in the shapes we just looked at to see this.

Triads can be 'decorated' by adding other notes to them. This produces a more colourful sound, and gives chords with names like 'major seventh' and 'minor seventh'. Let's look at some of these types of chords now.

Major6 and Major7 Chords

If we take a major triad and add the 6th note from the major scale, we get a '**major six**' chord. If we took a C major triad and added the 6th note in the scale, we would get **C6** (pronounced 'C major six').

Root	2nd	3rd	4th	5th	6th	7th
C	D	E	F	G	A	B

C6 = C, E, G, A

If this combination of notes sounds familiar, then it's probably because the uke is normally tuned G, C, E, A - the notes making up a C6 chord!

If we add the 7th note in the major scale to the major triad then we get a '**major seventh**' chord. Applied to the C major scale, we get a Cmaj7 chord (pronounced 'C major seventh' or 'C major seven').

Root	2nd	3rd	4th	5th	6th	7th
C	D	E	F	G	A	B

Cmaj7 = C, E, G, B

See these notes in the following chord shapes:

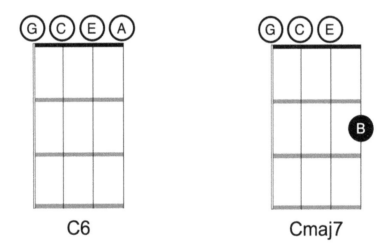

Both of these chords can be used to 'decorate' the sound of a basic major triad by using them as replacements. In other words, instead of playing C in a song, you could try using C6 or Cmaj7 instead. It won't always work, so use your ears and make your own mind up whether it sounds right or not.

There's one **big exception** to this principle: as a general rule major7 chords *don't* replace **major V** chords. It's a big no-no - the V chord needs to be a **major** or **dominant7** chord. This normally applies to any major stand-in chords too because as we've seen these are often performing some sort of V chord role in a song. Sometimes a major6 chord will sound ok as a V chord, but major or dominant7 is probably the best choice.

Before we look at both of these chord types being used in a progression, let's quickly look at decorating a minor triad.

The Minor7 Chord

If we add the **7th** note from the natural minor scale to a minor triad, we get a '**minor seventh**' or 'minor seven' chord, written using the symbol '**m7**'. The following diagrams show this being applied to the G natural minor scale to get Gm7:

G	A	Bb	C	D	Eb	F

Gm7 = G, Bb, D, F

The following chord shapes show the notes in Gm and Gm7. Compare the sound and structure of the chord shapes to see and hear the difference.

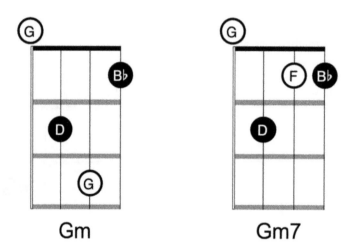

Gm   Gm7

In most situations we can use a m7 chord instead of a basic minor chord. For example, Dm7 could replace a Dm chord. We're going to look at an example of this right now.

Using and Learning to Hear Seventh Chords

We can use these more colourful chords to decorate simple chord progressions. Here's an example in the key of C. Play it using any basic chord shapes you know:

C – C – Dm - G7

We've already got a V7 chord in this example so we'll leave that chord alone.

The other chords can be played using the alternative chords as follows:

Example 11.1 (Audio Track 11.1)

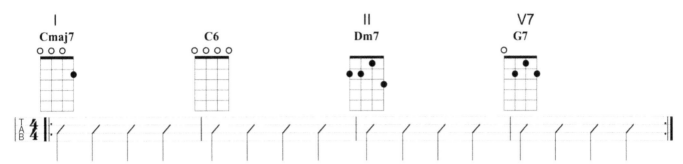

This kind of chord progression is common in jazz and show tunes, many of which are popular in the uke repertoire. Play it around a few times, listening carefully to the sound of the alternative chords. Compare them to the sound of the basic triads too, this will help you learn to recognise them.

A quick word about the C6 chord: the notes it contains are the same as in an Am7 chord:

C6 = C, E, G, A

Am7 = A, C, E, G

This means that you would very likely see the same progression written out with **alternative notation**, with the C6 chord being described as Am7 instead. This isn't that surprising when you realise that C6 and Am7 are closely related, being relative major and minor.

Don't let this confuse you, just be aware that sometimes the same chord or chord shape can be described using a few possible names. The name used will depend on the context it is being used in. For example, what note is the bass player in the band playing, what chord is the piano player playing... that sort of thing.

Here's Something Important

I want to make it really clear that we use seventh chords because of the **sound** they give us. You see, I don't want you to think that you have to use them just because you *can*. They're simply tools, we use them to create musical sounds - it's *not* about blindly following rules.

Try this Practical Exercise

Let's do a little exercise. Grab your uke and play the basic C chord we just used. Next, play the C major7 chord. *Listen* to the different *flavour* each of these two chords has. I think the major7 chord has a softer, 'dreamier' sound.

Hear how all these chords convey a different sound, mood or feel? Well, *this* is what determines which chord we'd use in a situation. In conclusion, use your theory knowledge, but always let your **ears** be the final judge and have the confidence to go with what you think sounds right, rather than just doing what someone like me tells you to do!

Other Seventh Chord Examples

The **major7** chord is quite distinctive and can really stand out in a progression, making it quite easy to hear and recognise. It's fairly common to change from a major triad to a major7 chord, this creates some movement in an otherwise static sounding chord progression. Play the following to hear C changing to Cmaj7 in the first two bars.

Example 11.2 (Audio Track 11.2)

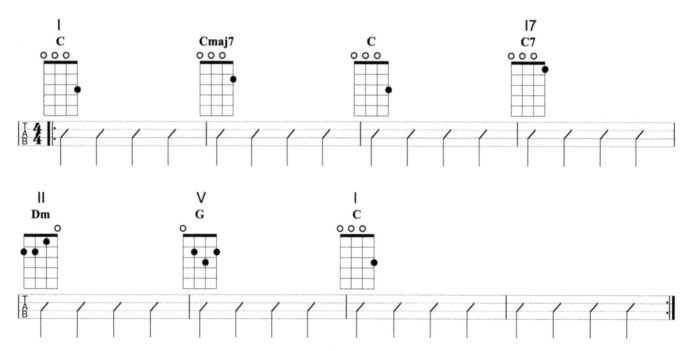

Later in this example you can see we're switching between C and C7, providing yet more movement and contrast. I've given you this example to highlight the different sounds C, Cmaj7 and C7 give us, but you do hear this idea used in songs. This particular one reminds me of 'Everybody's Talking' from the film 'Midnight Cowboy'.

Compare the sound of a minor7 chord to a simple minor triad using the Gm and Gm7 chord shapes from the next progression (example **11.3**).

How would you describe these two different 'shades' of the minor sound? To my ears, the **minor 7** chord is softer and more subtle. Spend a little time comparing and trying to really hear the different flavours of these chords.

When you're ready, try example **11.3** along with the audio track. Hear how nicely the Gm7 leads to the C7 chord? This is because of the way the notes move along the E string throughout the change. Pay attention to this small detail as you play the progression.

Example 11.3 (Audio Track 11.3)

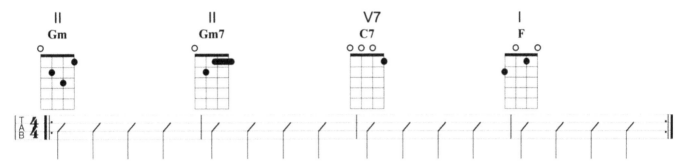

Here's another progression to try in the key of F major. Again, notice how the Gm7 (II) leads smoothly to the C7 chord (V).

Example 11.4 (Audio Track 11.4)

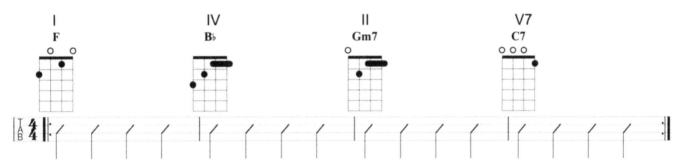

The way the notes in one chord flow into the notes in the next chord is called **voice leading**. This is a big topic and we don't need to go into it here, but being aware of how the individual notes in one chord connect to those in the next chord is worth paying attention to. It will help you decide on the best combinations of chord shapes to use and make your playing sound more musical and polished. By not just restricting our chord choice to plain major and minor triad chords, we open up all sorts of lovely sounding voice leading possibilities.

With voice leading, we're able to create little 'steps' between the chords in a progression. You can clearly hear this in the next example. Pay special attention to the descending notes on the 1st string, which show voice leading in action.

Example 11.5 (Audio Track 11.5)

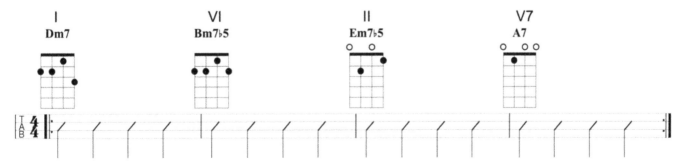

This example also introduces a chord we haven't looked at yet: the m7b5 chord (pronounced 'minor seven flat five'). Sometimes you may hear these called 'half diminished' chords, don't worry about why, just remember the alternative name for it.

As the name suggests, these chords are simply minor7 chords with a flattened 5th note. In the Bm7 chord, the 5th is F#. In a Bm7b5 chord this note is flattened by a semitone to become F.

The same applies to the Em7b5 chord: the 5th of Em7 (B) is flattened by a semitone to get Bb. You're unlikely to see many m7b5 chords, but if you do, you'll at least know a bit about them.

Try this Practical Exercise

Let's try a few of these chords in an arrangement of the ukulele favourite 'Fly Me To The Moon'. This contains a few chords we haven't seen yet, but don't worry about this, we'll cover them in a moment. The main point of the exercise is to give you practice combining some of the chords we've studied in this chapter. Also, listen out for the voice leading from chord to chord. Practice the example, playing it along with the audio track when you're ready. It's a lot of fun to play - enjoy!

Example 11.6 (Audio Track 11.6)

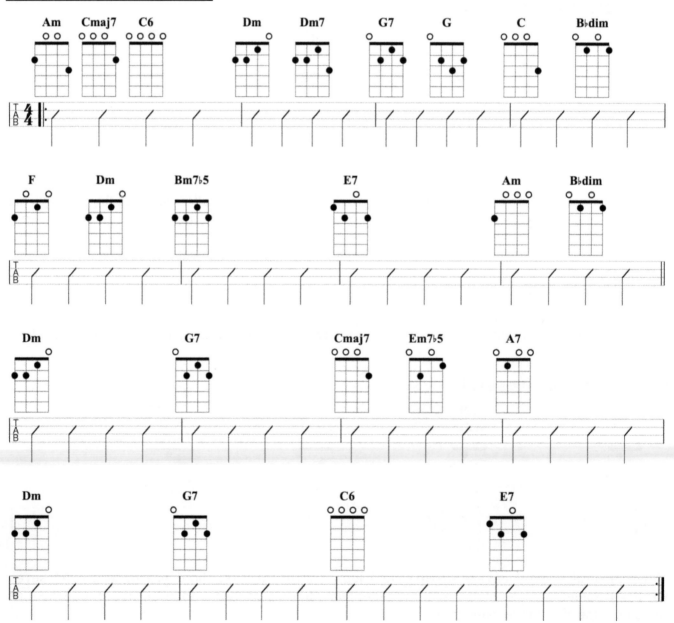

Diminished Chords

We saw in **Chapter 4** how diminished triads are chord VII in a major key chord family and how they form part of a dominant7 chord. You also learned the only diminished chord shapes you really need to know. Now we'll look at the way that diminished chords are often used in a piece of music.

Diminished chords are normally written using the chord symbol dim or o. For example: Cdim, Co, Fdim, Go etc.

Normally when we see a chord symbol in a song chart for a diminished chord, it's telling us to play a **diminished7 chord**. This is simply a diminished triad with an extra note added, and can be played using the two shapes from **Chapter 4**.

Many times when you see a diminished chord it is acting as a 'connecting' chord between two chords a tone apart. This has a lot to do with voice leading again, and in many cases a diminished chord will lead very smoothly from one chord to the next.

Play the next example and listen to how the transition from C to Dm is really enhanced by adding the C#dim chord. Spend a while playing bars 1-3 of this example to really soak up the sound. Remember, the purpose of this book is to help you recognise what you hear in the songs you play, so pay attention to the *sound* of these examples.

Example 11.7 (Audio Track 11.7)

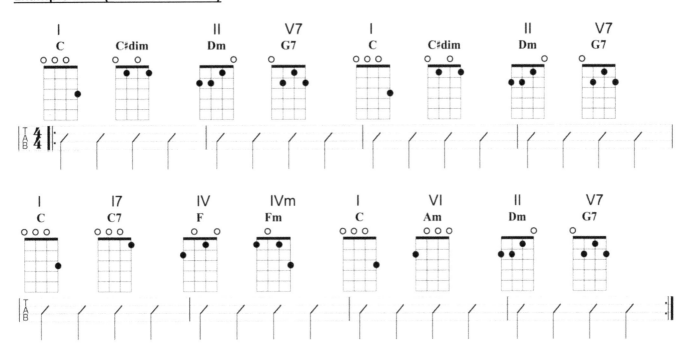

I'm sure you've heard this sort of distinctive chord progression before, the diminished chord creates a 'climbing' effect as it moves. Progressions like this, and diminished chords in general, feature in lots of jazz standards and show tunes, many of which have permeated the popular uke repertoire. Listen to anything by The Inkspots (a vocal group from the 1930) or standards like 'The Lady is a Tramp' or 'Ain't Misbehavin' to hear these kinds of chord sequences at work. And the next time you're at uke band practice and you play a song containing a diminished chord, look at it and see what it's doing. Is it functioning as one of these 'connecting' chords like we just examined?

Remember, *any* diminished chord you might need can be played using just *one* of the two shapes we saw in **Chapter 4**, so brush up on those diminished chords, you never know when you might need them!

'Suspended' Chords: The sus2 and sus4 Chord

We touched on these briefly in **Chapter 8**, but here's a little reminder...

A 'sus' chord is a chord which has had its 3rd *suspended*. This basically means that the 3rd in the triad has been (often temporarily) replaced by another note. If we replace the 3rd with the note below it in the parent scale, the **2nd**, then the major triad becomes a **sus2** chord.

Let's use a G major chord as an example. The notes in a G chord are G, B and D, the root, 3rd and 5th notes from the parent G major scale. The formula for **Gsus2** is shown in the following table. You can see the 2nd has replaced the 3rd.

Root	2nd	3rd	4th	5th	6th	7th
G	A	B	C	D	E	F#

In a **sus4** chord, the 3rd is replaced by the note above it in the parent scale, the **4th**. The formula for **Gsus4** is shown in this next table.

Root	2nd	3rd	4th	5th	6th	7th
G	A	B	C	D	E	F#

Now look at the following chord shapes to see how this theory applies on the uke.

Study what's happening on the A string. Of course, also listen to the sounds of these common chords so you can eventually recognise them when you hear them.

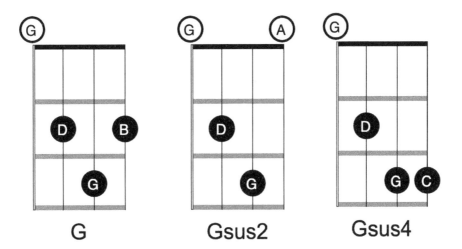

Listen to how the 2nd and, especially the 4th, sound like they want to return to the 3rd. Play the examples some more to really hear this effect, it's one of the trademark qualities of suspended chords.

We can easily get Dsus2 and Dsus4 chords by modifying the familiar D major shape. These are shown in the following diagrams. Notice how the 2nd (E) and the 4th (G) notes from the D major scale are replacing the 3rd (F#) in these shapes. Play these chords on your uke, and remember, listen carefully to the sound they produce.

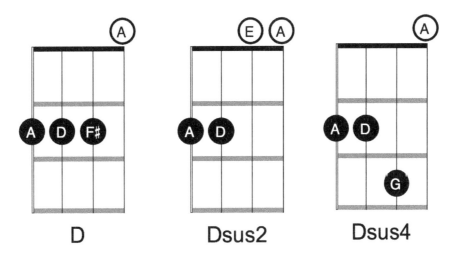

So, how are 'sus' chords used?

The general idea is that 'sus' chords are used to decorate major chords. Often they are played in conjunction with the 'non sus' version of the triad. Other times, the sus chords replace the major triad altogether. It just depends on what the composer/songwriter decides to do.

Now we have enough chord examples to make a little riff. This is how you'll frequently hear these chords used, often in intros, interludes or fills within a song.

Grab your uke and give the following exercise a play through. Try it along with the audio track too.

Example 11.8 (Audio Track 11.8)

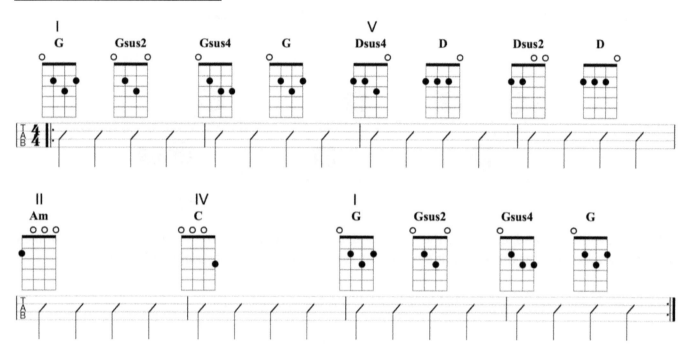

I'm sure you'll recognise the sound of major and sus chords used together, it's very common. Songwriters and composers often use it to bring colour and interest to a static major chord. Adding some sus sounds creates movement in the progression. By the way, sus chords can also be used in place of minor chords. Try using Gsus2 and Gsus4 with a Gm chord - it can sound great.

Try this Practical Exercise

Take a song you know which uses some D and G chords. Try replacing some of them with sus2 and sus4 chords. Experiment - you could stumble across some really cool sounds you didn't know about before.

Also, hunt out some other shapes for playing 'sus' chords. Any good chord reference book is a good place to start.

The Augmented Chord

There's one more type of chord we should look at and that's the **augmented** chord. The distinctive sound of augmented chords, whilst not that common, does occur in some frequently used chord progressions.

In music, the word 'augment' basically means to **sharpen** by a **semitone**. This explains the name given to augmented chords, you see, they are basically major triads with a sharpened fifth.

C major = C (root), E (3rd), G (5th)

C augmented = C (root), E (3rd), G# (#5th)

As I've already said, augmented chords have a very distinctive sound. Train yourself to recognise them by comparing them with a major chord using the following shapes. Remember the 'PLAY, LISTEN, HEAR' approach for this.

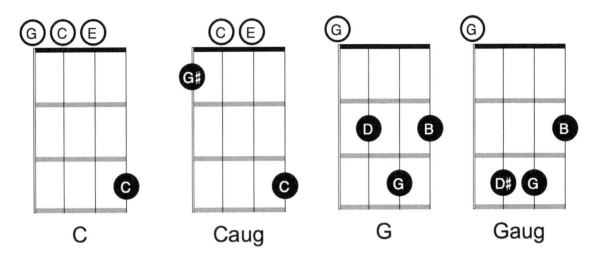

C　　　　Caug　　　　G　　　　Gaug

Can you spot the #5th in these chord shapes? It's G# for the C chord and D# for the G chord.

Often when you see an augmented chord in a song it's functioning as a V chord. This is happening in bars 2 and 8 in the next example.

Example 11.9 (Audio Track 11.9)

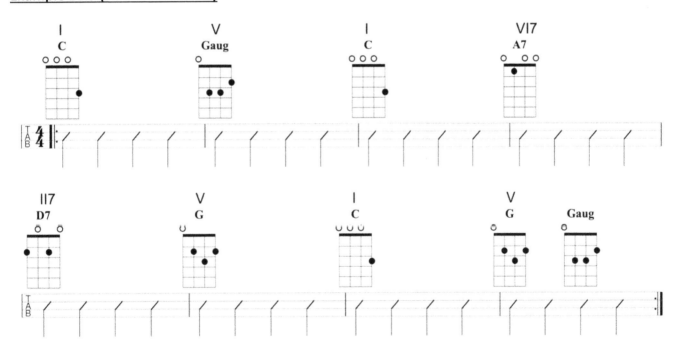

Hear how the augmented chord adds some more tension to the V chord, tension which is resolved when we return to the C chord.

Here's another example taken from the famous World War 2 song 'We'll Meet Again'. We're in the key of F major here, using a VImaj chord (D) as a stand-in. This is then changed to D augmented before resolving to the G7 (II7) chord. Again, you can hear the extra tension and movement the augmented chord creates in the chord progression. I've included a few moveable shapes in this example for you to practice. You can use other shapes if you prefer.

Example 11.10 (Audio Track 11.10)

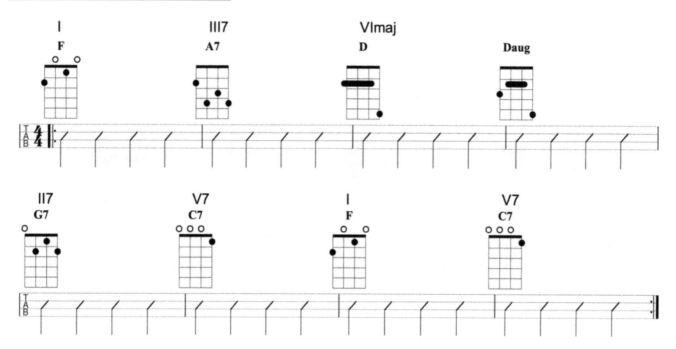

There's a specific chord progression you might hear which uses an augmented chord. I think of this as the 'ascending augmented' progression. The basic idea is that the 5th of a major chord 'climbs' in semitones.

You can see this happening in our next chord sequence: the C major chord becomes C augmented, C6 and C7, all because of the way the notes are moving on the 1st and 4th strings. Check out the chord diagrams to clearly see this happening. Play the progression to hear the sound we get, and when you're ready, try it along with the audio track.

Example 11.11 (Audio Track 11.11)

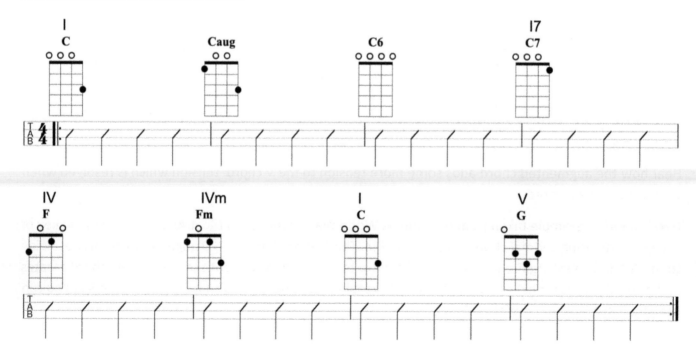

You probably recognise the sound of this chord sequence. It reminds me of 'The Greatest Love of All' (recorded by Whitney Houston and George Benson among others). Listen to this song, can you hear the 'ascending augmented' progression?

That's all for this chapter...

There are loads of other clever things we can do with basic chord progressions to get more complex sounds, but you're unlikely to come across them in most uke band situations. The purpose of this book is *not* to teach lots of advanced harmonic concepts, it's simply aiming to teach you to *listen* to the music you play and be able to understand at least some of what's happening. This will help you become more confident as a player and a musician, instead of simply playing from chord to chord on a song sheet without any idea of what's going on!

If you are interested in some of the more complex aspects of chords and chord progressions, then there is an abundance of great demos and explanations by lots of accomplished musicians on the internet. It isn't hard to find this information if you seek it out.

For now, check that you've grasped everything in this chapter. Play all the examples as much as you can, listen to the audio tracks, play along with them - do whatever you can to soak up these sounds and ideas so that your musical 'ear' becomes capable of recognising them. As always, test yourself with the questions that follow, and when you're ready I'll see you in the next chapter where we'll look at rhythm time-feel, strumming and more!

<u>**Quick Quiz**</u>

1. How do you build a **major triad** from a parent major scale? Which notes in the scale form the chord?

2. How do you build a **minor triad** from a parent natural minor scale? Which notes in the scale form the chord?

3. The G major scale is shown below. What are the notes in a **G major triad**?

   G A B C D E F# G

4. Which note in the parent scale is added to a major triad to turn it into a **maj7** (major seven) chord?

5. Using the notes in the C major scale shown below, give the notes in a **Cmaj7** chord.

   C D E F G A B

6. Using the notes in the A natural minor scale shown below, give the notes in an **Am7** chord.

   A B C D E F G

7. What do we do to a major triad to turn it into a **sus2** and **sus4** chord?

8. An **augmented** triad is like a major triad except for one difference. What is it?

Check Your Answers

1. *A major triad chord is built with the **root, 3rd** and **5th** notes in the parent major scale.*

2. *A minor triad chord is built with the **root, 3rd** and **5th** notes in the parent natural minor scale.*

3. *The notes in a G major triad are **G** (root), **B** (3rd) and **D** (5th), the root, 3rd and 5th in the G major scale.*

4. *The **7th** note in the parent scale is added to a major triad to turn it into a **maj7**. So the formula for a maj7 chord is **root, 3rd, 5th** and **7th** from the parent major scale.*

5. *The notes of a C chord are **C** (root), **E** (3rd) and **G** (5th). To make Cmaj7 we add the 7th, **B**. So **Cmaj7 = C, E, G, B.***

6. *The notes of Am7 are **A** (root), **C** (b3rd), **E** (5th) and **G** (b7th).*

7. *In a **sus2** chord, the **2nd** of the parent scale **replaces the 3rd** in the triad. In a **sus4** chord, the **4th** of the parent scale **replaces the 3rd** of the triad.*

8. *An augmented triad is like a major triad except that the **5th** is **sharpened by a semitone**. So, the formula for an augmented chord is **root + 3rd + #5th**.*

Chapter 12: Time, Strumming and 'Feeling' the Rhythm

The greatest chord progressions, the smoothest chord changing, and all the music theory knowledge in the world counts for nothing if a player can't play with at least a fairly solid rhythmic feel.

I'll be honest, some players *do* have an easier time than others when it comes to rhythm and strumming, they just seem to pick rhythms up quicker and can feel the rhythm of the music more naturally. But whether or not this is the case with you, I'm here to tell you this: by understanding and practicing some simple rhythmic concepts, *any* player can *improve* their sense of rhythm and timing *dramatically*.

That's the purpose of this chapter. We're going to talk about important rhythmic principles, practice some exercises and strumming patterns, and just generally get you thinking about and listening to how rhythm works in the music we play. I'm pretty certain that, no matter what stage you're at as a player, the material in this chapter will help you a lot.

So grab your ukulele, and let's begin.

Rhythmic 'Feel' and Strumming Patterns

One of the most frequently asked questions ukulele players ask is this:

What strumming pattern do I need for this song?

When I get asked this I have to stop and have a look at what I'm doing! You see, I'm not normally using any strumming pattern in particular, I'm just *listening* to the song and trying to fit in with it.

Don't get me wrong, strumming patterns are great tools, but there are no *rules* about which one to use, and in most cases it's fine to make up your own.

One exception to this is if the rhythm of the song is an important part of the its identity. In a song like 'You Really Got Me' by The Kinks, the chords need to be played as they are on the recording in order to sound like the song. Much of the time though, this simply isn't the case.

Another comment I've heard is:

I'm playing the right strumming pattern, but it doesn't sound like it should!

Strumming patterns on their own are just mechanical movements - playing the 'right' pattern won't necessarily make the song sound good. Strumming is simply the *method* we use to express the rhythmic 'feel' or 'groove' of a song to the listener.

To sum up, it all comes down to being able to hear the rhythmic 'feel' of the song. When we can do this, we can choose what sort of strumming rhythms to use.

Let's look at some things you can do to develop the ability to hear and feel the rhythm of a song. Relying on mechanical, pre-learned strumming patterns like many players do is fine for getting started, but I want to help you go beyond this.

Rhythmic Feel and 'Groove'

I'm sure you've listened to music and felt like you wanted to tap your foot, click your fingers, or move your body in some other way. Often we do this without even knowing it, it's just a natural response to music which has a great rhythmic 'feel' or 'groove' to it. Think of 'feel' and 'groove' as being like the rhythmic life, or soul, of the music. It's what makes it sound like music, instead of just a load of odd sounds and notes.

The chances are, you can easily hear and feel the groove in a piece of music, most people can. The problem is, the mechanics of playing the ukulele can inhibit this ability. It's almost like our brain shuts off our 'groove sensor' so we can direct all our brain power towards playing the instrument! So, if you have problems playing rhythms on your uke, *don't* think you've got no sense of rhythm and will never be able to play in time, you probably just need to get used to hearing the groove and performing the mechanical aspects of playing the ukulele at the same time. This largely comes down to practice and relaxation.

By now you're probably wondering what you can actually *do* to improve your sense of timing and rhythm, right? Read on.

Feeling the 'Beat' and Time Signatures

The 'beat' is like the 'rhythmic heartbeat' of a piece of music. When you clap your hands or tap your foot along with a song, you're probably clapping/tapping in time to the beat. It's like the *rhythmic pulse* underlying the whole song.

In most music the beat is felt in groups of **four**. This is called 'four-four time' and is written **4/4**. You'll often see 4/4 written at the start of a piece of music or on a song sheet as shown in the following image. When you do, it's telling you to play in 4/4 time and feel the beat in groups of four.

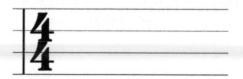

Most songs we play are in 4/4 time, and each bar of music lasts for four beats. Just knowing this can make it easier to keep your place in a song and follow a chord chart.

Sometimes we need to feel the beat in groups of **three**. This is called 'three-four' time and is written **3/4**. Sometimes you'll also hear it described as 'waltz time'. You might see 3/4 written at the start of a piece of music as shown in the following image. This tells you to play in 3/4 time and feel the beat in groups of three.

'Four-four' and 'three-four' time are both examples of **time signatures**. The time signature of a piece of music tells you how many beats are in each bar and how to count them (i.e. in groups of four, three, or whatever).

Try this Practical Exercise

Let's hear the difference between these two time signatures.

Put your uke down, and listen to any of the audio tracks that came with this book (except for **10.8**). Count along in groups of four ('1,2,3,4 - 1,2,3,4 etc'). You're counting in **4/4** when you do this. Try to really *hear* the beat of the music. Don't be in a hurry to play along on your uke, just *listen* and try to *feel* the beat.

This listening exercise is powerful - it's how we 'internalise' the groove so we can naturally hear it when we play.

When you're ready, grab your uke and play along to your chosen audio track. Perhaps you can hear and feel the beat and groove of the music better than before? Can you stay in time with the track more easily?

Try this Practical Exercise

Audio track **10.8** is in **3/4** time. Listen to it now and see if you can hear the three beats which make up each bar of the example. As before, don't play along yet, just listen and count in groups of three. Try to really *hear* the beat of the music and the groups of three.

When you're ready, grab your uke and play along to the audio track. Does anything feel different?

Hopefully you felt something change after doing both of these exercises, almost like your ability to sense the beat and groove suddenly improved a little. If not, don't worry, it soon will. I suggest repeating these exercises a few times *every* time you practice. They're simple, but the best practice methods often are!

Also, listen out for and count the beats in the music you hear in your day-to-day life, on TV, on the car radio etc. The more you do this, the more quickly your rhythmic ability will improve.

Common Rhythms and Strumming Ideas

Now that you understand some rhythmic fundamentals like **beat**, **groove** and **time**, we'll look at some common ways we play rhythms in music. These can be thought of as different rhythmic 'flavours' or 'feels'.

You may have heard musicians talk about things like 'swing feel', 'straight feel', 'shuffle feel' and wondered what they meant? If so, then keep reading because we're going to get into some of these next.

Some rhythmic ideas are difficult to describe in words - you need to hear them - so make sure to listen to the audio tracks which go with each example. I've made sure everything is easy to hear on these.

Now, instead of grabbing your uke and diving straight in, I suggest you do the following for **each** of the rhythmic feels we examine:

1. *Listen* to the audio track lots of times first! Get an imprint of how it's supposed to sound before you try and play it. You'll be amazed what a difference this makes. If you don't know how it sounds, how are you going to play it?
2. Count along as you listen. Most examples are in 4/4 time
3. Vocalise the rhythm using basic syllables like 'da, da-da, da' or whatever. It doesn't matter what it sounds like, it's just a way to hear, internalise and feel the rhythm you're going to play before you try to play it
4. When you're ready, put on the audio track and play along on your uke. Keep going and try to stay with me. If you make a mistake, try to recover and continue

One more **important** thing. The strumming patterns I give you are examples only. They'll work great in lots of situations, but they are by no means the definitive patterns for these rhythmic feels and there are many other options. I suggest you master my patterns, then experiment with them, changing them to create some variations of **your own**. This will really help you to build the ability to hear what works rhythmically in almost any situation, and automatically play the right kind of thing (wouldn't that be cool!).

I'm writing out the strumming patterns using the following notation:

D = *down* strum

U = *up* strum

There are other ways to write them out, but this method will work fine for now. Of course, listen to the audio tracks to hear them too.

Ok, let's look at some different rhythmic feels and see how we can play them on the uke.

Swing Feel

Many pop/jazz/blues songs are played with a *swing feel*. This can be heard in the music of people like Glenn Miller, the early pioneers of rock 'n' roll, as well as any blues artist.

As with many rhythmic feels, it's hard to describe what a swing feel sounds like, but the beat has a distinct 'bounce' to it. The easiest way to hear it is to compare it to a 'straight' feel, in other words a rhythm which isn't played with a swing feel.

Let's do this now, we'll use the following chord sequence for this:

Example 12.1 (Audio Tracks 12.1 and 12.2)

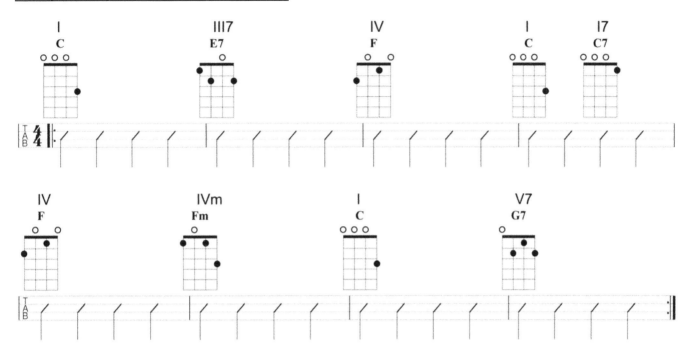

Listen to **audio track 12.1** to hear this played with a **straight** feel. Hear how the beats are all 'even' and of uniform length. It sounds musical, but maybe a bit mechanical.

The strumming I'm using for this example is shown here:

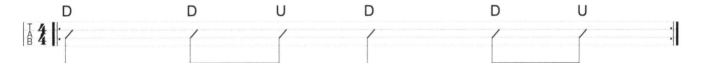

Now listen to **audio track 12.2** to hear the same chord progression played with a **swing** feel. The whole 'feel' of the track and the way all the instruments are playing is really quite different to the straight feel. It has a looser, less 'rigid' sound to it.

I'm actually strumming the same pattern as I did for the straight feel, but I'm interpreting it in a different way. Instead of the down-up strums on beats 2 and 3 being even, the down strummed note lasts for *longer* than the up-strummed one. This is the basis of the swing feel, but again, you need to hear it for it to make sense so listen to the audio demo. Anyway, the strumming is shown in the following diagram. The circled symbol at the start of the example is sometimes written on a piece of music to tell you to play it with a swing feel. Often it's missing, but now you'll at least know what it means if you ever do see it.

Listen out for the swing feel being used in many popular songs we play on ukulele. Standard songs like 'Fly Me To the Moon', 'All of Me' and 'The Lady Is a Tramp' are just a few you might come across. Also listen out for it being used in songs by artists like Buddy Holly and Elvis Presley.

Shuffle Feel

Another common 4/4 rhythmic pattern is a 'shuffle'. This comes in different forms and can be played with a straight feel or a swing feel. Again, it's hard to describe but tends to have a sort of 'bluesy' or 'rocky' feel.

Here's a 12 bar blues in the key of G. Listen to the audio track to hear the basic shuffle feel.

Example 12.3 (Audio Track 12.3)

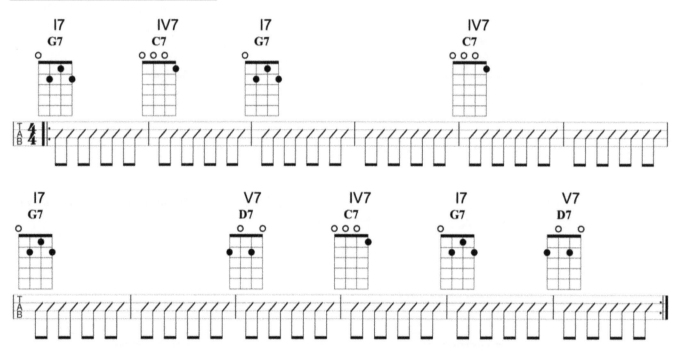

I'm basically strumming down-up on each beat here, but because it's played with a swing feel, the notes I play with the down strums are lasting for longer. Listen to the audio to hear this. To really nail the shuffle feel, we can emphasise the down strums on **beats 2** and **4** slightly.

In musical terms, we would call this **accenting** beats 2 and 4. Try it once you've got the basic pattern flowing nicely. The strumming is shown in the following diagram.

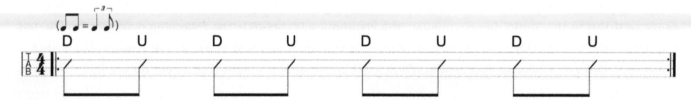

Shuffle rhythms can also work well when played with only down strums. It gives them a heavier, rockier sound which works particularly well when playing a straight shuffle feel.

To try this out, let's play the same chords as example 12.3, but with a **straight** shuffle feel using the following downward strumming pattern. Listen to audio track **12.4** to hear the sound before you try and play along.

Example 12.4 (Audio Track 12.4)

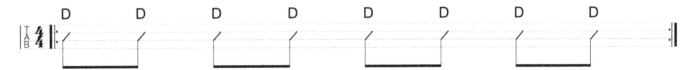

To hear a straight shuffle listen to songs like 'Johnny B Goode' by Chuck Berry or 'Rockin' All Over The World' by Status Quo, two classic examples of the shuffle rhythm at work!

'Train' Feel

'Train' rhythms are common in many country songs and have a forward-moving, 'driving' feel, hence the name! These are played with a straight feel and sound great on the uke.

Let's look at two examples of train rhythms.

The first one sounds like 'dum-dum-diddy-diddy'. This might sound silly, but these kinds of 'nonsense words' are a great way to remember different rhythms. Listen to the audio track of this example, and play along when you're familiar with the rhythmic pattern. This might remind you of 'City of New Orleans', a popular song in the uke repertoire.

Example 12.5 (Audio Track 12.5)

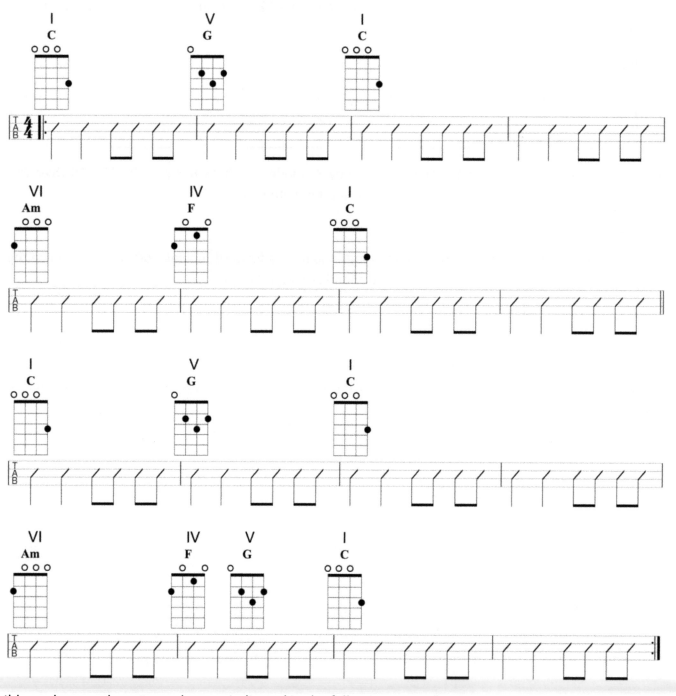

I'd use down and up strums here as indicated in the following example.

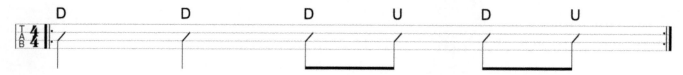

This next train rhythm has even more drive to it. I hear this one as 'dum-diddy-diddy-diddy'.

It works great for popular uke band songs like 'Folsom Prison Blues' by Johnny Cash. Listen to the audio and play along when you're ready. The strumming is shown below the chords.

Example 12.6 (Audio Track 12.6)

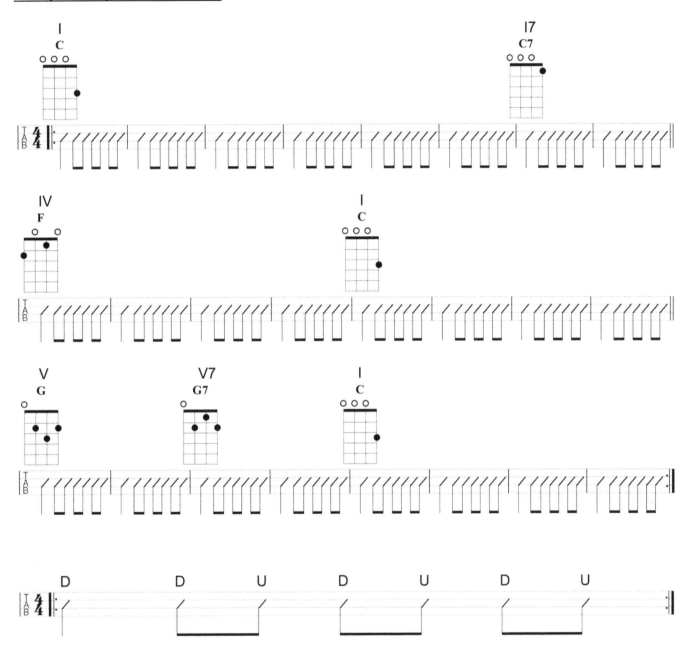

Remember, these rhythms need to 'drive' the song. Play them with finesse, but don't hold back - they should sound like a 20 ton locomotive steaming down the tracks!

Waltz Feel

We mentioned **3/4** time or waltz feel earlier in this chapter. Now I want to show you a couple of useful strumming rhythms you can practice and play. These aren't complicated, but they'll work nicely in most of the waltz songs you're likely to come across. Remember, listen to these examples carefully before you try and play them, this will help you to capture and express the 3/4 time feel in your strumming.

The first example is a simple 3/4 pattern which you need to know. We're strumming down on beats 1 and 3, and strumming down-up on beat 2. Try to accent beat 1 slightly and make the other strums slightly softer, this will give your strumming a solid 3/4 feel.

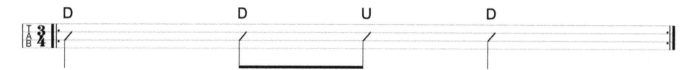

Apply this rhythm to the simple chord progression that follows. Often we play with a swing feel in 3/4 time, and this is how I'm performing this chord progression. Listen to the audio to hear the sound of this effect, and when you're ready, play along with me.

Example 12.7 (Audio Tracks 12.7 and 12.8)

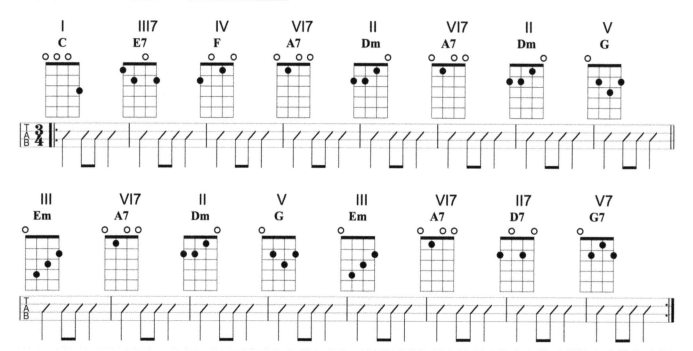

A simple variation of this pattern is to play down-up on beat 3 as well.

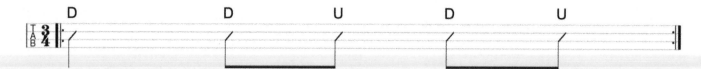

Listen to this being used on **Audio Track 12.8**. The chords are the same as in the previous example, so follow those again, just play this strumming variation. These patterns are pretty versatile and will work in lots of 3/4 and waltz time songs. So get them under your fingers and you'll be ready the next time somebody pulls out a waltz at uke band practice!

The Latin Feel

'Latin' rhythms are mainly associated with the music of Brazil and other South American countries, but they've crept into all sorts of other styles, from pop to jazz to country. The Latin feel I'm going to show you is not an authentic Latin rhythm such as a rhumba or bossa nova, but it's enough to give a song a Latin feel when needed.

This rhythm incorporates a 'rake' strum. This is where the strumming finger or pick, 'rakes' down across all four strings individually, creating a distinctive percussive sound. It's hard to describe in words, so listen to the audio track for the next example to hear how it should sound. It's probably going to take a little practice to get the hang of the rake, it needs to be controlled and in time, but with practice it will soon feel quite easy.

We'll try the Latin feel over a single A major chord to start with. It's written out in the following diagram, with the rake shown as an arrow. This diagram might not mean much until you hear the rhythm though, so listen to the audio track too.

Example 12.9 (Audio Track 12.9)

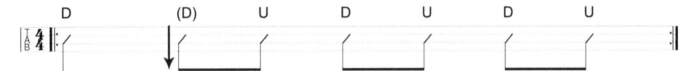

When you've got the rhythm happening, try applying it to this longer example based on the traditional song 'O Sole Mio'.

Example 12.10 (Audio Track 12.10)

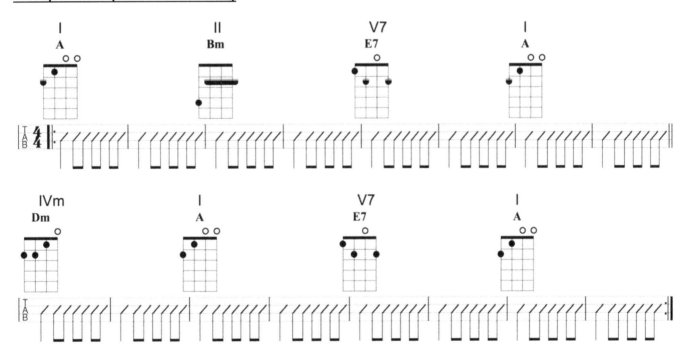

Sometimes I like to use this rhythm for songs which originally had a different feel altogether. A good example is 'Will You Still Love Me Tomorrow', a big hit in the 1960s. The following chord progression is similar to this song. Remember, listen to the audio track to get a really good idea of what it should sound like *before* you try to play it. It's tempting to jump straight in, but a bit of careful listening first often leads to more successful results.

Example 12.11 (Audio Track 12.11)

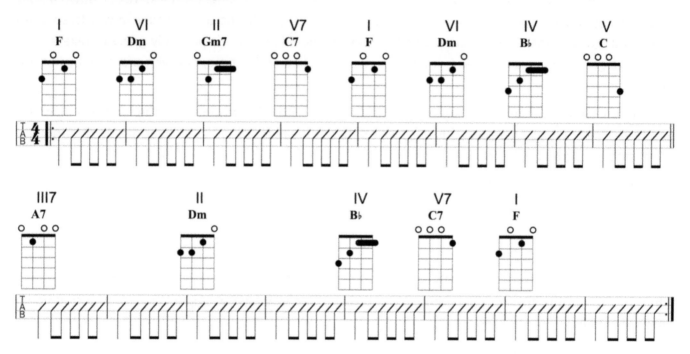

I think this rhythmic feel is a lot of fun to play around with, and it can work great in lots of 'non-Latin' songs. Look for opportunities to use it in songs **you** play, it could give some of them a whole new lease of life!

Putting it all Together

Hopefully these different rhythmic styles have given you some ideas when it comes to playing songs. As always, the key is simply to **listen** carefully to the song you want to play and try to pick out the rhythms at work.

Is the song using a swing or straight feel?

Is it in a 3/4 or 4/4 time signature?

Would a driving 'train' rhythm work, or does it want more of a laid back shuffle feel?

With experience and familiarity with these rhythmic feels, plus a lot of listening, you'll quickly become more skilled at choosing a rhythm feel which will fit well with a song, even when playing something you've never played before.

Listen also to the *dynamics* (energy levels) of the song. Music without dynamics is like someone speaking in a flat, monotone voice - it's hard not to switch off!

Things to listen for could be:

Does the song get more lively in some places and more gentle in others?

Does it have pauses or stops where no strumming is required?

Are the verses played more softly than the chorus?

These little things can have a big impact on how good you make your playing and performances sound.

Before we wrap up, here's a final example using a mix of rakes, strumming and swing feel. It illustrates how a simple chord progression can be decorated by varying the playing techniques you use. Have a careful listen to the audio example (**audio track 12.12**) before we discuss a few performance tips for playing it.

In the **verse** try using the **Latin feel** we looked at:

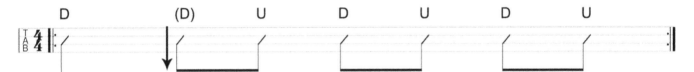

To create some contrast, we'll play the **chorus** with a **swing** feel, using the swing strumming idea from earlier:

You might want to practice each of these sections before you join them together, then when you're ready, put on the audio track and play along using the chords shown in the following diagram. Good luck!

Example 12.12 (Audio Track 12.12)

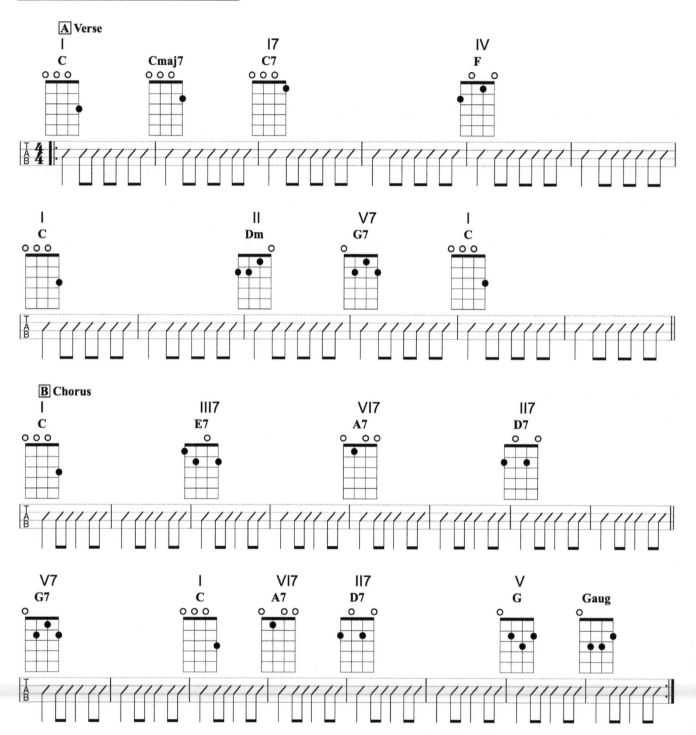

That's all for this chapter...

Rhythm is an enormous topic with almost *endless* possibilities, but hopefully this chapter has opened your eyes and ears to some of the different rhythmic feels we can use on the ukulele.

At the risk of repeating myself, the most important thing is to **listen** and try to absorb the different rhythmic feels we hear in the music around us. You don't need to be an expert on rhythm to do this, a basic idea of how something sounds is enough.

As you become more experienced, try to analyse the rhythms a song uses as a musician, rather than just a listener. This will help you become comfortable playing all the different rhythmic variations you may need to play.

Above all, don't forget to focus on the fundamentals of rhythm, things like learning to hear the beat and keeping your playing from speeding up or slowing down. Playing along with the audio tracks which come with this book can help you a lot with this skill.

So I hope this chapter has been helpful. Spend time with the exercises we've covered here (you can't just do them once and expect miraculous results!), and when you're ready head to the final section in this book where we'll wrap everything up.

Final Words

I said in the introduction that this book is intended as a 'roadmap' to help you develop your ability and grow your confidence as a player, so that you can enjoy playing the uke more than ever before. Now that we've reached the end, I hope that you feel it has got you on track to doing this!

Of course, there's no way to cover everything in a book like this, but hopefully what I've shown you has made you think differently about how you listen to and play the music you enjoy.

I know from my own experience what a difference the material in these lessons can make to our playing, so dig in and explore everything thoroughly. One day you'll look back and be amazed at how much progress you've made.

We are fortunate today that there are some amazing resources on the internet to learn from. As well as songs, strumming patterns and ukulele-playing techniques, you can find some fascinating explanations about how chords and songs work. These will complement this book nicely, so feel free to continue your journey of discovery on your own – it'll be much easier and less confusing with the knowledge you've gleaned from these pages.

Above all, as I've said multiple times, **listen**. The more you can improve your ability to hear and recognise the building blocks of music like chords, progressions and rhythms, the more your playing will improve and the easier and more enjoyable making music with others will become.

Remember too that you can never master all the material here. Even the greatest musicians often say they still feel like beginners! The process of becoming a good musician is about constantly trying to learn more and improve. If we do so, then we can't help but see results. So whilst we've reached the end of this book, it's really just the beginning, and I'd encourage you to now go back over this material and work with it some more. Do this, and you'll start to understand it on a whole new level.

That's all from me for now. Thanks for coming along with me on this musical journey. Good luck and happy music making!

David Shipway

Music Theory
for Ukulele

My first book, **Music Theory for Ukulele** is *the* book for any ukulele player who wants to quickly and easily unlock the music theory knowledge that all uke players need to know... without it taking years of confusion, frustration and expensive lessons!

It's the perfect companion to **Next Level Ukulele**, taking you deeper into some of the most important music theory topics you need to understand.

- 11 bite-sized, easy-to-digest chapters, covering essential topics like the major scale, notes on the ukulele fretboard, chords, major and minor keys, common ukulele chord sequences and much more
- Test your understanding with quizzes (answers provided!) and use practical exercises to see, play and understand how the theory applies to the ukulele
- Ukulele fretboard diagrams and chord boxes make everything easy to apply to your uke.
- Absolutely no music reading necessary
- Includes free supporting website where you can watch and hear video demonstrations of selected exercises from the book played up close

You'll find it in most online stores or by ordering from your local bookshop.

Appendix 1

This diagram shows you all the notes on the ukulele fretboard. Use this to help you move things like chord shapes around easily. This diagram applies to any uke in standard tuning (G-C-E-A).

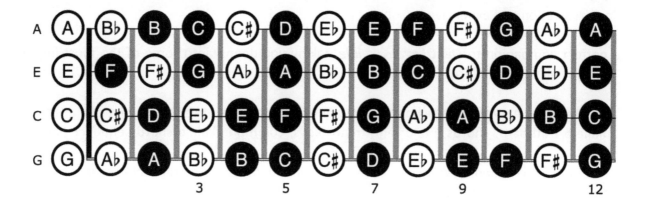

Appendix 2

This chart shows you all of the twelve major key chord families.

KEY	I	II	III	IV	V	VI	VII
C	C	Dm	Em	F	G	Am	Bdim
F	F	Gm	Am	Bb	C	Dm	Edim
Bb	Bb	Cm	Dm	Eb	F	Gm	Adim
Eb	Eb	Fm	Gm	Ab	Bb	Cm	Ddim
Ab	Ab	Bbm	Cm	Db	Eb	Fm	Gdim
Db	Db	Ebm	Fm	Gb	Ab	Bbm	Cdim
Gb	Gb	Abm	Bbm	Cb	Db	Ebm	Fdim
B	B	C#m	D#m	E	F#	G#m	A#dim
E	E	F#m	G#m	A	B	C#m	D#dim
A	A	Bm	C#m	D	E	F#m	G#dim
D	D	Em	F#m	G	A	Bm	C#dim
G	G	Am	Bm	C	D	Em	F#dim

Appendix 3

This chart shows you all of the twelve minor key chord families.

In each key the V chord is shown as minor, but remember it's often played as a major or dominant7 chord!

KEY	I	II	III	IV	V	VI	VII
A minor	Am	Bdim	C	Dm	Em	F	G
E minor	Em	F#dim	G	Am	Bm	C	D
D minor	Dm	Edim	F	Gm	Am	Bb	C
G minor	Gm	Adim	Bb	Cm	Dm	Eb	F
B minor	Bm	C#dim	D	Em	F#m	G	A
C minor	Cm	Ddim	Eb	Fm	Gm	Ab	Bb
F minor	Fm	Gdim	Ab	Bbm	Cm	Dd	Eb
F# minor	F#m	G#dim	A	Bm	C#m	D	E
C# minor	C#m	D#dim	E	F#m	G#m	A	B
Bb minor	Bbm	Cdim	Db	Ebm	Fm	Gb	Ab
Eb minor	Ebm	Fdim	Gb	Abm	Bbm	Cb	Db
G# minor	G#m	A#dim	B	C#m	D#m	E	F#

Note: sometimes chords in minor chord families are labelled with Roman numerals which are slightly different from those shown in this table. This doesn't matter, just be aware that some teachers and books might use these variations.

Next Level Ukulele
by David Shipway

Published by Headstock Books
headstockbooks.com

Copyright © 2022 David Shipway

Paperback ISBN: 978-1-914453-75-5
Hardcover ISBN: 978-1-914453-77-9 / 978-1-914453-78-6
Ebook ISBN: 978-1-914453-76-2

Milton Keynes UK
Ingram Content Group UK Ltd.
UKHW051512161023
430705UK00018B/433